MOON ENERGY
for Beginners

SIMONE BUTLER

An Introduction to Moon Spells, Lunar Phases, and Rituals

NEW SHOE PRESS

Inspiring | Educating | Creating | Entertaining

Brimming with creative inspiration, how-to projects, and useful information to enrich your everyday life, quarto.com is a favorite destination for those pursuing their interests and passions.

First Published in 2022 by New Shoe Press, an imprint of The Quarto Group,
100 Cummings Center, Suite 265-D, Beverly, MA 01915, USA.
T (978) 282-9590 **F** (978) 283-2742 Quarto.com

New Shoe Press titles are also available at discount for retail, wholesale, promotional, and bulk purchase. For details, contact the Special Sales Manager by email at specialsales@quarto.com or by mail at The Quarto Group, Attn: Special Sales Manager, 100 Cummings Center, Suite 265-D, Beverly, MA 01915, USA.

ISBN: 978-0-7603-8013-0
eISBN: 978-0-7603-8014-7

The content in this book was previously published in *Moon Power* (Fair Winds Press 2017) by Simone Butler.

Library of Congress Cataloging-in-Publication Data available

Illustration: Fay Miladowska

Contents

Introduction 4

1 What Is Moon Power? 6

2 Your Inner Goddess 17

3 Moon in Aries 25

4 Moon in Taurus 36

5 Moon in Gemini 46

6 Moon in Cancer. 56

7 Moon in Leo 67

8 Moon in Virgo 78

9 Moon in Libra 88

10 Moon in Scorpio 98

11 Moon in Sagittarius 108

12 Moon in Capricorn 119

13 Moon in Aquarius 129

14 Moon in Pisces. 140

Questions for Reflection and Journaling 152

Recommended Reading 153

Websites for Teachers Featured in this Book 154

About the Author 155

Index 158

Introduction

You're about to learn the art of personal Moon magic! This isn't a difficult process. Magic, quite simply, is about your feelings and desires and how you direct them toward a particular goal. Connecting to the Moon—both within and without—provides the magical conduit.

Moon worship has always come easily to me, as I have four planets (including my Sun) in Moon-ruled Cancer. Late one night many years ago, I climbed up a steep hill in Malibu, California, to commune with the Full Moon. There she was, huge in the sky, her unearthly light shimmering through drizzling rain. At that moment, I felt a deep primal connection to her and all of life. Through letting the Moon guide you, you too can have profound experiences, like mine.

Based on where the Moon was located on the day you were born, your Moon sign shows your emotional nature and what makes you feel secure. It also reveals the wisdom you've accumulated in previous lives—and where you can get stuck in ruts. The Moon is a rich source of information and, should you desire, you can learn a lot about your personal Moon by getting your birth chart done so you can better understand the wisdom she holds for you. However, for now we'll keep things simple by focusing on the Moon's characteristics in different signs and her Goddess associations.

It's easy to determine where the Moon was on the day you were born. Find out your time of birth if possible, as you may have been born on a day the Moon changed signs (which it does every two-and-a-half days). Then consult my site at www. astroalchemy.com to discover your Moon sign.

I draw from many cultures to help you celebrate the magic of the New and Full Moons. But much of what I'm sharing comes from my own inner guidance. I follow the Wiccan path of my Celtic ancestors, but I've included rituals in this book inspired by many different paths. Times have changed, and it's essential to flow with those changes. That's why I'm big on creating your own traditions, taking the best of the old and adding what works for you. Where ritual is concerned, something simple and heartfelt is better than an impressive ceremony that doesn't really touch your soul.

Although mountaintop epiphanies are wonderful—and you're sure to have some as you develop a relationship with the Moon—I've come to also value mundane experiences: Lighting candles on my altar to bless the day. Creating New Moon collages to invoke what I want for the month ahead. Drawing the Full Moon's radiance down into my body. Paying attention to nature's synchronistic messages—an escaped hare on Easter, a giant tortoise strolling the sidewalk at a Taurus Moon. Yes, I've experienced those moments of magic. You will, too, as you start working with your Moon Mama.

Throughout these chapters, I'll offer suggestions for altars you can create for each Moon sign. You can leave them up for the month at hand—or longer if you choose. Altars are the heart of magical work. An altar is a collection of meaningful elements put together in pleasing ways, infused with your emotions and intention. Whenever you mindfully select an alter's objects and lovingly and intentionally put them together, the altar becomes imprinted with the feeling of what you're trying to create. This could be greater courage, prosperity, a new relationship, or whatever else you need. Each time you use your altar, you affect the world around you through the power of suggestion.

You can do the rituals in the following chapters at the New and Full Moons, or whenever you desire. For example, if the Taurus Full Moon ritual sounds appealing, look up when that Full Moon falls and wait for it, or do it sooner, ideally when the Moon is in Taurus. This is especially effective if Taurus is your personal Moon sign. Doing ritual on the day the Moon is in your Moon sign generates extra-powerful magic.

To increase something (such as love or money), perform your ritual when the Moon is waxing (New Moon to the peak of the Full Moon). Waning Moons (after the Full Moon's peak until just before it's New) are for banishing things, such as excess weight or unwanted suitors.

How to Perform an Effective Ritual

- Get clear on your intention.

- Set up an altar that reflects your intent, if you choose.

- Approach the Goddess reverently and ask for her help. She needs an invitation to enter your life!

- Affirm the highest and best outcome for all concerned.

- Remain confident that the ritual will work.

- Keep your focus steady until you've completed the ritual.

- Express gratitude.

- Stay open to intuitive promptings.

You may need patience to find your footing with performing rituals. It might feel uncomfortable or scary at first, especially if you had a strict religious upbringing. Your rusty priestess instincts may need a little oiling to function smoothly. Joining with like-minded sisters will help. Women are strongest in the collective, when we bond and share with one another. And ritual is a prime way to do that. Why not join or start a circle of women devoted to the Goddess? Or, you could host a New Moon or Full Moon party with your female friends. Some Full Moon rituals are geared toward communal participation.

You could also take turns hosting and honoring different Goddesses. For each event, a different person researches a Goddess of her choosing. She then creates a ritual and craft activity to share. Once you get in the habit of doing ritual, whether alone or in a group, your connection to the Goddess will come alive—and so will your life! May you reunite with your inner Goddess in ways that deeply satisfy your soul!

PART 1

What is Moon Power?

You have only to stand under a Full Moon to feel her power. The Moon is a living being! The seas dance with her as tides ebb and flow. Your body undulates with her in your monthly cycles and passionate embraces. On some level, you sense this primal feminine power—especially if you've participated in the greatest mystery of all, bringing a soul to life. Even if you've never given birth, however, the Moon is here to remind you of your innate womanly nature.

Perhaps you've sensed the Moon's comforting presence at her dark phase near the New Moon, as you mourned a loss and struggled to accept. Or maybe the Full Moon's radiance helped bring you back to life. Dark, full, or in between, the shape-shifting Moon is your conduit to a higher power—a connection that can never be broken. It's an ethereal yet durable umbilical cord to your soul, that mysterious larger part of you that intersects with all creation. That's why I'm capitalizing Moon in this book, to give our cosmic mother the honor she deserves.

Since ancient times, women have felt this magical lunar bond. The Moon is our "vein of gold," our access point to the core of creation. Identifying and honoring your lunar nature helps you feel comfortable in your skin.

Unfortunately, our culture's focus on the rational mind and a remote, masculine God has separated us from nature and the divine feminine, our true spiritual source. Yet rest assured that the Great Goddess is returning (in fact, she never left!). The fact that you are reading this book shows you're a vital part of this change in consciousness. Basically, it's a shift from the head to the heart. We've dwelt too long in a mind-dominated realm, and we've all suffered greatly for it. Now we're learning to open our hearts and trust our intuition. Caring for others—and our Earth—has become crucial to our survival.

Embracing your Moon will help you make this shift from head to heart. On your day of birth, the Moon was moving through a specific part of the heavens. Knowing its location on that date unlocks the secret code to your primal nature and gifts.

The Moon's powerful vibration made a certain imprint on you, based upon your soul's history. For instance, if the Moon was in Aries, you may have had many lifetimes as a warrior. Your soul is encoded with bold, independent Amazon energy. If the Moon was traveling through Pisces, however, you've walked a spiritual path in many lives. Your soul carries the glamour of the Mystic. We'll take a look at each sign's past life correspondences later in this book.

In her book The Vein of Gold: A Journey to Your Creative Heart, Julia Cameron describes the vein of gold as an indestructible connection to the divine that we all have—in other words, our spiritual DNA. In the same way that our physical DNA gives us specific traits and potentials, the vein of gold constitutes a one-of-a-kind imprint of our creative gifts and spiritual potential.

As an astrologer, I see this blueprint of our gifts as the natal chart. That's the map of the heavens on the day you were born, which shows all the planetary players and how they interact with each other. Learning how to interpret this chart takes years of study and observation. But fortunately you can know a great deal about yourself just by reflecting on your natal Moon—perhaps while reverently standing under the Full Moon.

Astrologer Dana Gerhardt has given much thought to communing with the Full Moon. "For much of my adult life," she says, "I've stood awkwardly under Luna, trying to lasso her with my modern mind, vaguely wanting something more than I was getting." After years of trying, she finally found a method that worked. "You have to sink your awareness lower than mind," she confides. "It's a relaxed and spacious state. The Moon becomes a bell whose ringing brings you into the field of the Mother, where body and soul can quietly drink."

Luna and The Soul

Reflecting the light of our life-giving Sun, the Moon represents the qualities in us that are reflective and responsive rather than assertive and proactive. Though men also have a receptive side and some feel a strong affinity with the Moon, Luna is a soul mate for women—reflecting back to us our deep, natural intuitive qualities.

Yet long neglect of the feeling realm and minimization of the feminine have put us at odds with both our soul and our planet. Some even say we're at "one minute to midnight" in terms of our ability to rebound. Climate change, for instance, has brought us more intense hurricanes, typhoons, heat waves, and droughts that affect our food supply. Our cosmic mama is dearly hoping we'll wake up and turn things around before it's too late.

This turnaround cannot happen from a strictly rational place. All the scientific reports in the world can't heal global warming, even if they do raise awareness. What's needed at this pivotal point in history is for us (both men and women) to reconnect with our instinctual wisdom and let it inspire us to act. Maybe that looks like quitting your corporate job and starting a nonprofit organization to create change. You might invest in cutting-edge technologies to clean up the ocean, move closer to the land, build an energy-efficient home, or raise pesticide-free vegetables. Or maybe you could organize weekly meditations to mobilize healing.

Turning within is a good place to start. There are powerful healing energies encoded deep inside you that have an uncanny correspondence to the planets. You don't have to know astrology to tap into and use these regenerative forces, although it helps. Just by getting to know and honor your inner depths, you begin to heal yourself and the world.

It's time to bring forth our feminine souls. Way back in the fifteenth century, philosopher Marsilio Ficino asserted that we must put soul at the very center of our lives. Our individual soul, he said, is inseparable from the world's soul. It connects us to a broader realm related to fate and destiny. Ficino believed that the soul is not meant to be understood, but honored for the magic and meaning it brings to us.

Wise Blood

Women are inextricably linked to the Moon. Our first calendars were based on the Moon's twenty-nine-and-a-half-day cycle, which mirrors the menstruation cycle. The words *moon*, *month*, and *menstruate* come from the same root. Even the phrase to be "on your Moon" (meaning to menstruate) reflects this connection.

In ancient times, when the Moon disappeared each month, she was said to be retreating from the outer world to honor her blood flow. Likewise, tribal women retired to menstrual huts to bond with one another and do ritual during their red flow, when their instinctual body wisdom was at its greatest. It was a time to rest from daily activities and an opportunity to get in touch with emotions and instincts. Some cultures, however, were frightened by women's heightened powers during this time. To be able to bleed and not die was seen as powerful magic. Women on their Moon were thought to disrupt the daily activities of the tribe, so the people in charge made menstruation taboo and seclusion mandatory.

Astrologer Donna Cunningham, in her wonderful book *The Moon in Your Life: Being a Lunar Type in a Solar World*, states that modern women ignore their special needs during menstruation at their peril. The menstrual cycle, she says, is essential in helping us integrate the lunar side of our nature and lunar hemisphere (right side) of our brain. "The emotional changes we go through at menstruation," she says in the book, "are part of a natural mechanism for regulating our emotions. If we cry, if we explode, we are discharging toxic feelings that could do damage if not released."

Cunningham cites author Louise Lacey's research in Lunaception, which confirms that tribal women menstruated at the dark Moon and became fertile at the Full Moon. Even today, when women begin living together, their menstrual cycles often synchronize. Lacey believes that before artificial lighting began to interfere with our pineal glands, which regulate our cycles, the brightness of the Full Moon triggered ovulation. Since many women strongly feel their sexual mojo when they ovulate, it's no wonder that ancient Full Moon festivals were so wild.

To make it in the modern world, most of us suppress our lunar nature—especially at "that time of the month." Scheduling a couple of rest days each month to honor your red flow will go a long way toward balancing your body-mind. Remember that your menstrual cycle is the source of your deepest intuition—a great blessing, rather than a "curse."

Whether you're still menstruating or have shifted into the crone phase of life in which your body's retention of wise blood now sources your power, you're still a sister of the sacred red flow. You can use the dark Moon to channel this energy in ways that bring you power and peace.

Why The Moon?

Let's take a closer look at Luna. How is it that this rocky, barren orb became associated with everything from divine feminine mysteries and passionate love to werewolves and madness?

To understand our history with the Moon, you have to imagine a much earlier time, long before traffic noise and electric lights filled the night. Thousands of years ago, when we lived in agrarian societies, the Moon was Queen of the Night. When Luna was in her dark phase (near the New Moon), nights were ominous. Humans were vulnerable to creatures with hungry bellies. But when Luna was in her glory at the Full Moon, couples indulged in passionate trysts, and herbs were harvested to maximize their potency.

Back then, we knew instinctively that we were one with Mother Nature. Our sacred essence had not yet been torn away from us. We worshiped the Goddess through fertility rites and ceremonies that connected us to our natural source and affirmed our oneness with nature. For example, each year at the sacred holiday known as Beltane (now called May Day), people slipped out to the forests or fields and "fertilized" them through coupling. For one day, marriage vows were cast aside and instinct ruled. Any children born of these unions were considered holy and special.

Every culture had a Moon Goddess to whom people prayed for bountiful crops and healthy children. In fact, sometimes the Moon was considered even more important than the Sun. Vedic astrology, still practiced throughout India and parts of the West, is Moon-based. Ancient shrines to Moon Goddesses worldwide still emit intense vibrations generated from thousands of years of worship.

Farming by the Moon phase is a time-honored practice. The ancients found that planting and harvesting at certain lunar cycles yielded better results than at others. Although this can vary by region and climate, the Old Farmer's Almanac recommends planting above-ground flowers and vegetables during the Waxing Moon (from the New Moon to the Full Moon) and below-ground crops, such as flowering bulbs and root vegetables, during the Waning Moon (from the Full Moon to the New Moon).

The Full Moon also transmits mysterious energies that evoke strong feelings. Who knows how many love poems were inspired by the Full Moon, and how many babies have been conceived during this ultra-sensual time? Animals go wild howling at the Full Moon (hence the myths of werewolves and

ALIEN EXPERIENCES

You'd think that a heavenly body with such an effect on our feelings and physical forms would be teeming with life. Yet when Apollo astronauts first landed on the Moon, they found it barren. Still, they felt the lunar magic—many had uncanny experiences, including a crew who heard strange, unearthly music while traversing the dark side of the Moon. Some, such as Edgar Mitchell, had spiritual awakenings. Others seemed shaken and scared by whatever they had experienced while in space.

The Moon is a magnet for all kinds of bizarre theories. An episode of Ancient Aliens on the History Channel suggested that Luna is a hollow alien watchtower of sorts that was towed into the orbit of the Earth . . . and that the dark side of the Moon conceals a station (which would account for the sounds heard by astronauts). It's rumored that there was a time on Earth before the Moon existed, so who knows—perhaps the Moon we hold so dear is actually a creation of our galactic brethren!

vampires). A 2011 study published in the journal PLOS ONE found that African lions are indeed more likely to attack and kill humans around the Full Moon. Domestic dogs and cats are also at risk. As reported in the July 2007 Journal of the American Veterinary Medical Association, a study of 11,940 cases at the Colorado State University Veterinary Medical Center found the risk of emergency room visits for these pets (ranging from cardiac arrest to trauma) to be 23 percent higher for cats and 28 percent higher for dogs near the Full Moon.

Luna in the News

Luna's messages are not just for ancient stargazers or astronauts. Our cosmic lunar companion is continually broadcasting to us, often at an unprecedented rate. In these turbulent times, when we're all looking for guidance, many of us are starting to pay closer attention to what Luna is trying to tell us (even if it may come from aliens!).

Millions tuned in to NASA's live stream of the Blood Moon–Super Moon–lunar eclipse on September 27, 2015, and millions of others viewed the dazzling spectacle overhead in the night sky. The Moon was burnt orange—and so big you could almost touch it!

What did it mean? Super Moons (when the Moon is extra close to the Earth, and therefore, larger than usual) are not uncommon; nor are lunar eclipses, which occur about twice a year. However, a total lunar eclipse is rare, and even rarer at a Super Moon. To put things in perspective, a series of four total lunar eclipse/Blood Moons will not happen again until 2033.

Such events have often coincided with powerful endings and beginnings. At the latest one (April 15, 2014, to September 27, 2015) many anticipated the worst; in fact some ministers pronounced this Blood Moon tetrad to be the beginning of the "end times" foretold in the Bible.

Yet life went on, albeit altered for some. Think about your own life during that period—no doubt some big changes occurred. A woman told me her life changed profoundly when she reconnected with a karmic mate at the first Blood Moon; each ensuing eclipse of the cycle brought him back into her life until at the final Blood Moon the relationship imploded. She was heartbroken but liberated, grateful that the karmic lesson was finally complete.

Spiritual sources proclaimed the most recent Blood Moon tetrad to be a harbinger of a new Earth, as our solar system enters an unprecedented phase in which space and time are morphing. Many claim that the devastation we're witnessing represents the death of old, ego-driven ways—the last gasps of a dominant patriarchy giving way to a culture that honors the divine feminine once more.

LUNAR ECLIPSE

Lunar eclipses (when the Sun eclipses the Moon, causing Earth to cast a shadow on her) are the most powerful time for practicing magic, says Dorothy Morrison in Everyday Magic. Yet they are not the only dance that Luna engages Sol (the sun), her cosmic mate. Sometimes she turns the tables and eclipses him—blocking him at least partially from view. Partial solar or lunar eclipses occur every six months; total eclipses are much less frequent—and tend to have stronger effects. If eclipses of either variety hit a sensitive point in your natal chart, they're apt to bring major turning points. Eclipses often require us to let go of the old in order to make room for the new.

Moon Phases

The Sun and the Moon are the primary players in Earth's cosmic drama. Since the Sun is active, or yang, he's cast in the masculine role. The Moon is receptive, or yin, and fundamentally feminine. We'll explore the mythic relationship between these eternal lovers in the next chapter.

The Moon revolves around the Earth, revealing different views of herself. We never get to see her dark side, though. A woman is entitled to her privacy! Since Luna doesn't radiate her own light but reflects the Sun's, each night she distributes a different amount of his light according to their varying relationship.

Over the course of a month, Luna goes from backstage (invisible, but still quite powerful) at the

Waning Crescent and New Moon to the radiant star of the cosmic show when she is full. She goes through eight Moon phases each month altogether, each with its own characteristics. Goddess-based cultures saw Luna's monthly journey as her transformation from Maiden (fresh, young waxing New Moon) to Mother (pregnant, illuminating full phase) to Crone (wise, elderly, waning dark Moon).

Knowing your Moon phase reveals fascinating things about your soul's journey. However, it's only one piece of a far bigger puzzle represented by your astrological chart. Some of the qualities listed on the four following pages may resonate with you, and others may not. Your Moon sign and many other factors also come into play. You can find your Moon Phase at spacefem.com/quizzes/moon.

New Moon

When Luna joins Sol (the Sun) at the dark of the Moon, they plant seeds to create new life. Like all conceptions, this phase is spontaneous and passionate. If you're born at a New Moon, you'll try anything once—or even twice!

Born when the Moon was dark, you've learned to live in the moment and go on instinct. You respond impulsively and immediately to events, and are apt to possess a magnetic star quality. Like pioneering artist Georgia O'Keeffe, who was born under a New Moon and spent years living alone in the New Mexico desert, you enjoy your solitude and may be perceived as too self-focused or lacking objectivity. But you came here to be who you are and give your gifts to the world. You're learning to trust your heart over your head, and to use your tremendous imagination to further a cause that's larger than you.

Waxing Crescent

At this phase, your drive to experience life grows even stronger as the Moon waxes toward full. This phase is associated with the Maiden, a young woman who experiments with becoming an individual. As your faith in yourself as a powerful woman grows, you'll find it easier to express your true self and navigate relationships wisely.

Hope in the face of darkness is a key theme for those born under the Waxing Crescent. Nineteen-year-old Joan of Arc should have been celebrated for her spirited actions in saving France from English domination during the Hundred Years' War. Yet this courageous young woman was burned at the stake, and only received her canonization much later.

If you were born at this Moon phase, follow your instincts and know that you're doing important work. If compulsive behaviors plague you, channel them into worthy endeavors that will live on after you're gone.

First Quarter

The First Quarter Moon person thrives on action and challenge. You're a wild woman, uninhibited in your expression of sexual, spiritual, and creative goals. First Quarters are often seen running marathons, saving lives in emergency rooms, or fighting wars.

Often in this phase there is conflict with the powers that be. Aretha Franklin, for example, had her share of run-ins with authority. Early in her career, she severed her secure but stifling relationship with Columbia Records to make a fresh start, and soon shot to stardom with her passionate anthem, "Respect."

If you were born at this Moon phase, you're here to tear down old structures and create new ones. Don't be afraid to blaze a trail or stir up a little trouble. But taking a diplomatic approach may be more effective than willful or impatient action.

Waxing Gibbous

If you were born at the Waxing Gibbous phase, you strive to be the best you can be. You may try hard to reach a goal but feel you've fallen short. Try to relax and enjoy the process, and praise yourself for small steps in the right direction. You've learned that it takes a village to create change; teaming up with others increases your impact—and your enjoyment of life.

You're enormously creative and growth-oriented, and you use your analytical mind to plot a course of action before you commit. You stick with people

LUNAR CRAZIES

It's no coincidence that the Moon's powerful correlation with oceanic tides also affects our bodies. More hurricanes and tornadoes occur at New and Full Moons than at any other time, and since our bodies are at least 60 percent water, we also go through turbulence. Perhaps you've noticed that it's harder to fall asleep when the Moon is full. In a 2013 Swiss sleep research project involving thirty-one subjects, people took longer to nod off at a Full Moon; they also slept twenty minutes less and spent 30 percent less time in deep sleep mode. And it wasn't just due to the Moon's brightness—the studies took place in rooms with zero exposure to outside light.

and causes you're passionate about through thick and thin.

Generous to a fault, you invest a great deal in your relationships. Cutting your losses is tough for you. Nicole Kidman, born under this moon, ended her marriage to Tom Cruise despite her deep love for him. Yet loss made her stronger. With her Moon gathering strength on its way to fullness, she grows ever more luminous as she matures.

Full Moon

Ever feel like you're always in the spotlight? If you were born at a Full Moon (when Luna and Sol were opposite each other), the Moon is illuminating you. Everyone can see your fabulousness and foibles.

You have a strong urge to make your mark on the world. Many Full Moon types shoot quickly to fame and fortune based on their over-the-top talents, desire to be seen and heard, and powerful magnetism. Quite a few of the modern Moon Goddesses profiled in this book were born at this phase. They embody the sensual, romantic nature of the Full Moon.

Because you're so connected to others, it's hard for you to be objective. You need other people to reflect you back to yourself, but seeing their point of view may be a challenge. Also, people often project their fears and fantasies onto you. Consequently, your relationships can be quite dramatic. You're willing to go to extremes for whom or what you cherish. Ultimately, though, you need to cultivate balance.

Waning Gibbous (Disseminating)

You are a gifted communicator, eager to tell your truth and engage in spirited discussions. Like healer-activist Mother Teresa, you have an important message to give the world and work tirelessly to share it.

The lure of the outer world and its trappings is starting to wane at this stage. Even though you're still drawn to exciting crusades, you sense there's something more, and you're determined to find out what it is. You've learned a lot about relating, and can be counted on to be a loyal companion. That doesn't guarantee marital success, though. Princess Diana never found the happiness and security she sought. Yet she did find kindred spirits, and her big heart made millions of people love her.

Try to cultivate detachment so you're not buffeted to and fro by circumstances. Finding an important message to share will help you create a meaningful life. You are a born teacher; the world needs to hear your voice.

Last Quarter

In this phase, you're on a mission to find a new path. There might be a "crisis in consciousness," as old ways become less meaningful and new ones call to you. Set aside regular time to connect with your soul and listen to its wisdom. Striving too hard to earn others' approval only causes frustration; your own approval is all you need at this point.

The Last Quarter person often carries a whiff of tragedy. Like soulful singer Billie Holiday, born under this phase, you deeply feel the sadness of the world. As the Moon wanes back into the darkness from whence she came, you may feel a sense of impermanence or aloneness, as if you no longer belong here, and the next world is calling you. There's no reason to conform to others' expectations; your inner self will just rebel. Simply be yourself.

You may be perceived as mystical, ahead of your time, or even downright strange. Who could have foreseen the remarkable impact of a girl from Mississippi with the odd name of Oprah? Embrace your dream. As long as it's heartfelt, this Moon phase can pull strings to make it come true.

Waning Crescent (Balsamic)

When the Moon reaches this final phase of her cycle, being "normal" is no longer an option. You are the guru, the elder, the Wise Woman. You have strong psychic abilities and can sense the presence of spirits. You may even be seen as a prophetess. Your rich inner life is the source of much delight, but those who don't understand may call you a dreamer, lost in your own little world. Staying grounded is essential for you.

Your sensitivity and deep feelings can seem like a burden, but they also feed your extraordinary creativity. Like Frida Kahlo and her compelling art, your creative gifts often reflect your personal pain. Despite the pain, you're driven to express your unique vision.

This lifetime is about karmic completion. You may have intense, short-term relationships with those you've known in other lifetimes, so you can clear your slate and start fresh. Learning to detach from (but not deny) painful memories will help you avoid escapism or addiction. A too-busy life that doesn't include quiet solitude won't serve the needs of your magnificent soul, which needs time and space in which to flourish.

———————

Now that you know your Moon phase, you have a better understanding of what stage you've reached in your soul's evolution. You can couple this insight with what you'll be learning later on about your Moon sign to more fully flesh out your lunar identity. But first, let's take a look at how you can cultivate your inner Goddess and share that magical energy with your partner.

PART 2

Your Inner Goddess

Science has proven we are made of the very same particles and atoms found throughout the cosmos. We are stardust. Although modern man needed this to be proven, ancient civilizations knew it intuitively. They sensed those twinkling heavenly lights impacted us personally—and none so profoundly as our nearest cosmic companion, the Moon.

Luna remains a great mystery to us—almost as mysterious as our own inner depths. Although the Moon exists in the three-dimensional world (an extension of the waking mind, or left brain), she also engages with the dreaming mind, or right brain. This is the realm of myth, magic, and metaphor. In this mode we can sense the invisible, speak in dreams to loved ones long dead, and find meaning in even the most disturbing events. Learning to cultivate and feel comfortable in the formless right-brain space is one key to discovering and honoring your inner Goddess.

As you tap into your Moon, that deep well from which you drink, you access the wisdom you've absorbed in this and prior lives. Because it reflects your subconscious self or soul (the part of you that endures after death), your Moon holds all your memories dating back to the start of creation. These memories are more like feelings and impressions, rather than facts. They're the source of your inborn ability to play the piano, calculate math problems in your head, or know exactly what to say to someone who's grieving.

Yet the Moon is also the hidden part of you that has trouble healing, the place where you went as a child (and still go) to hide when you didn't feel safe. It also represents your knee-jerk reactions to things. It's you at your most vulnerable—and most genuine.

The Feeling Realm

Your feelings are the most reliable conduit to the intuitive right-brain realm. To coax out your inner Goddess, start letting your true feelings rise up and find expression. This can be tricky if past attempts at speaking your truth were rejected. By nature, women are emotional beings. But the culture we've lived in for the past few thousand years has taught us to disown our nature—to pretend we're calm when in fact we're terrified, to act like things are copacetic when in fact we're outraged.

Not only do we shame ourselves for having a hard time "keeping a lid on it," but we've even learned to judge each other (as well as our children) for being too emotional. Although there are times when tempering your feelings may be necessary (such as when driving a car or operating on a patient), trying to constantly keep your emotions at bay is as futile

as attempting to prevent the Moon from waxing toward full.

We need to learn to accept and love all aspects of our nature, and regain the confidence that comes from owning our feelings. I once had an acting teacher who stressed the importance of "playing all 88 keys, as on a piano." He likened this musical metaphor to our repertoire of feelings and constantly sought to stretch our emotional range. He'd throw us into improvisational scenarios: "You're a brother and sister and your mother just died. Go!"

What this practice taught me was the importance of getting out of my own way. If I hesitated for even a second, trying to figure out how to play the scene, I'd come off as wooden and artificial. But if I went on instinct, the results were often raw and moving.

I also learned something remarkable about my Goddess nature. One time at the end of class, after a grueling but exhilarating emotional workout, the teacher turned to me and said, "Simone, I want you to go around to each person and say something to them." Again, if I'd hesitated I would have been lost. But luckily I'd learned my lesson. I don't recall what I said to each classmate; it didn't seem to matter. A mantle of power had descended over the group. We were outside of time for who knows how long. By the end, we were all in tears.

Without intending to, I'd called down the Goddess. Or you could say, I'd called forth the Goddess within. My willingness to be spontaneous and real had opened the doorway for her to walk through. And by the way, there's nothing particularly special about me. You too can call forth the Goddess—in fact, that's what this book is all about.

Getting in touch with the Goddess is not always hearts and flowers, however. Sometimes being real with yourself means tapping into deep, dark emotions you've bottled up for decades or even centuries (the darkest stuff often has past-life origins). You may consider emotions such as rage and jealousy shameful. But why would your Mother Goddess give you these feelings if you weren't meant to express and release them?

Thinking of the divine as female may contradict the religious teachings you were raised on, but the true face of God is feminine. Somewhere along the line, we seem to have forgotten that mothers birth babies, not fathers—and the same is true in the divine realm. Fathers have their place, of course, and we need to honor them as well. But it's past time to remember that our wombs (along with the rest of us) are sacred.

In astrology, the Moon signifies your personal mother—or at least how you experienced her. Whether you had a hard time with your mother or adore her to the ends of the Earth, your Moon sign and the aspects it makes will tell the story. Most astrologers believe that we've lived before and that we chose our current mothers and fathers. Even if your mother is difficult, she's still a carrier of certain "medicine" you couldn't get in any other way. To the extent that you can accept and forgive her, you'll have greater access to your personal Moon magic.

In the time of the Great Mother Goddess, roughly from 7000 B.C.E. to 3500 B.C.E., the Moon and the Mother were one in the same—and a woman's emotional nature was celebrated as divine. People lived in mostly peaceful agrarian societies. But around 3000 B.C.E., the God began to grow more powerful. Eventually, the patriarchy overtook the matriarchy, leading to the burning of tens of thousands of women, or possibly more, at the stake as witches. To fully understand this shift, see Riane Eisler's comprehensive book, The Chalice and the Blade. In it, she states that we're returning to an era of feminine power—but this time in divine partnership that honors the masculine as well.

Women have come a long way since the Burning Times, but we still tend to ignore or suppress our feelings. Not wanting to appear irrational or weak, we measure ourselves by a masculine yardstick— trying hard to get ahead while putting our lunar needs on the back burner. Often it's not until our feeling nature rebels and we're beset with chronic fatigue or worse that we slow down long enough to reassess our approach to life.

The Pleasure Connection

What has become of our inner Goddess? Many of us aren't even aware that we have one, or how to get in touch with her. She may show her face on date night, when clad in your sexiest outfit, you feel connected to a certain primal power. Or perhaps you feel her after a particularly satisfying day at work, as you relax with your favorite glass of wine. But it's easy to let whole days go by without taking a minute to honor her.

Regena Thomashauer of Mama Gena's School of Womanly Arts says that modern women are missing a vital nutrient, the lack of which holds us back in countless ways. That nutrient is pleasure. As Thomashauer notes in her latest book, Pussy: A Reclamation, cultivating joy and pleasure on a daily basis is absolutely essential to a woman's fulfillment. Not only does it banish stress, she says, but it also connects us to our divinity.

The word pleasure often conjures up images of sex, but there are many forms of sensual pleasure. Smelling a rose or biting into a ripe, juicy peach can make you swoon. Whatever takes you out of your head and into your heart will bring you bliss and rejuvenate both body and spirit. To embody the Goddess, you must make a point of enjoying your life. Be present in your body and breathe into your aches and pains. Embrace your sensual nature.

Being connected to your inner Goddess requires an awareness of your second chakra, just below the navel. This is the locus of your sexual and emotional power. It is your womb space, the place in you that knows what you want and isn't afraid to go after it. It's your pleasure center. Yet for many of us, there is great fear and constriction around this chakra. You may experience problems with your gut or feel ashamed of the belly fat you carry—perhaps as a protection against unwanted intrusion. Many of us are still holding on to sexual wounds that have caused us to shut down our second chakra and lose access to our primal power. Breathing deeply into this chakra on a regular basis will help center you and clear away old blockages so you can feel more pleasure.

Dealing with Moods

Although some men are getting better at expressing their intuition and emotions, women are still considered the "sensitive" gender. This is a mixed blessing for those with a strong lunar nature (especially if you have several planets in Cancer or a prominent Moon in your natal chart). Although you may experience rapturous, mystical feelings that elude others, you may also be perceived as needy or unstable. Perhaps you grew up hearing, "Don't be so

sensitive" or "I'll give you something to cry about." So you stuffed your feelings down to get by.

Feelings, however, don't take kindly to being stuffed. The Moon will have her way with you. She communicates through your moods. Something minor irritates you and suddenly you're furious. You're probably overreacting due to a backlog of unexpressed anger or sadness that's desperate to find an outlet. You must forgive yourself for not knowing how to express your moods. No one ever taught you.

How best to deal with a mood? By giving it a healthy outlet. Psychologist Carl Jung believed that moods are messengers from our subconscious mind and want to give us vital information (such as what we're really feeling). Rather than trying to ignore the mood, he said, it's better to give it a voice: Write, draw, sing, or dance it. Yell it at the top of your lungs or punch a pillow! Or do some rituals such as those in this book. Ritual will connect you to something larger—the Divine Mother—and calm, ground, and heal you. Once the mood is acknowledged, it will leave you in peace. Just be sure to look for whatever gift it left behind.

Until you start to honor your feelings—especially the "irrational" ones—emotional health will likely elude you, and your body will continue to rebel by sending you signals in the form of tension, pain, or illness.

Luckily, an explosion of ancient spiritual practices, such as ritual, meditation, fire-walking, and dream work, can help you reconnect to your Moon, or interior life (what my yoga teacher calls "your inner atmosphere"). Paying attention to your feelings and inner life has not been encouraged in our culture until recently, and it's still a new concept for many. Understanding your own personal Moon and how to work with lunar cycles (which you'll learn about later in this book) will help you access your inner atmosphere and feel more connected to the divine feminine that lives within you.

One good way to awaken the divine feminine within is to travel to places where the Goddess was once worshiped—especially if they reflect your personal heritage. If you have Celtic ancestry, for instance, making a pilgrimage to England's Glastonbury Tor or the Scottish highlands could rekindle ancient memories.

Many women have had profound experiences while exploring the sacred sites of southern France, where Mary Magdalene was said to have lived after fleeing the Holy Land. A priestess of Isis, Mary was much more than just one of Jesus's followers—and many believe she was not a prostitute, as the early Church claimed. And thanks to Pope Francis, who in June 2016 elevated St. Mary Magdalene's July 22 memorial day to a feast day, the Catholic Church is finally recognizing her as equal to the other apostles. For a revealing look at her extraordinary life and relationship with her beloved, see *The Magdalen Manuscript* by Tom Kenyon and Judi Sion.

If you're lucky, you may even receive a message from the Goddess while visiting a sacred site. It happened to me on a pilgrimage to the Oracle of Delphi in Greece. At this ancient shrine, the priestess as Oracle once channeled divine messages. Drawn down a flight of steps to the catacombs beneath the ruined temple, I laid my hands on the cool, earthen walls. An undulating wave of ecstatic energy filled me. "Give this energy to men," the Goddess commanded. "Don't judge them, just love them."

Your Sexual Power

For some of us, seeing sexuality as spiritual may be difficult to do. Yet sexual energy is as natural as the Sun and Moon. What a tragedy that women as far back as the biblical Delilah have been vilified for their powers of attraction, accused of being the ruin of men. We are in fact the saviors of men—capable of healing, fortifying, delighting, and even enlightening them. But we must first learn to trust our deep sexual powers—especially if they've gotten us into trouble in the past.

Think about your first sexual experience. Was it wondrous and fulfilling? If so, you were fortunate. Many women bear lifelong emotional scars from careless or cruel early sexual experiences. If this is true for you, uncovering your inner Goddess may take a little extra time and attention. She was likely buried under painful feelings you weren't able to process at the time that need to be unearthed and released.

Unfortunately, there are still places in the world where a woman can be stoned to death or otherwise denigrated for expressing her sexual nature. But we in the West are privileged to live in a time when pretty much anything goes. It's no longer against the law to engage in certain sexual acts, nor does having a child out of wedlock carry the stigma it once did. Now you can marry your same-sex partner, or even find acceptance as a transgender woman, as Caitlyn Jenner did. We still have a long way to go in terms of full LGBT acceptance, but great strides have been made.

No matter your age or sexual persuasion, you're now free to pursue what turns you on—and to find

BECOMING THE GOD AND GODDESS

Becoming the Goddess to your partner isn't as difficult as you might think. Every woman has this ability, as does every man to become the God. You don't have to be in a committed partnership to work this ritual, but monogamy does create a sacred container without which many women can't fully let go. Either way, safety is important. And, make sure your partner is open and willing to go with the flow.

Full Moons are ideal for awakening the God and Goddess, as our bodies and emotions are at high tide, giving greater access to expanded states. But the dark Moon can also be powerful, or any time that feels right to you.

The process is simple:

- Retire to your cozy bedroom. Light candles on either side of the bed, and banish all phones and electronic devices. Burn your favorite incense or diffuse a soothing scent to set the mood.
- Sit cross-legged on the bed, holding hands and looking into each other's eyes. Relax and feel love for your partner as you breathe together deeply.
- When you're ready, release your right hand and place it over your partner's heart. Say, with conviction, "I see the God in you."
- Let this sink in. Then, release your hand from your partner's heart and place his hand over your heart. Breathe together.
- When ready, he replies, "I see the Goddess in you."
- Surrender to the energy that takes you over. There's no need to guide the lovemaking, unless either of you receives a strong directive. Trust the Goddess to transport you to new worlds!

your cosmic mate, if you choose. Despite the proliferation of porn on the internet that leads us to believe we must be sexual acrobats or have perfect bodies to attract a partner, many men seek a more heart-centered, spiritual–sexual connection. One great way to meet them is by going to Tantra events, also called pujas, in which men and women come together to honor the Goddess in safe and pleasurable ways. Be sure to start with a beginners' group featuring nonsexual touch, which will help you stretch just slightly out of your comfort zone. Also, make sure the facilitator enforces strong boundaries among participants so you can relax, knowing you're safe.

Even if pujas aren't your thing, you can still practice connecting to your second chakra and breathing into your power center. Once you've forged a solid connection to that place where your inner Goddess resides, you'll feel more centered and calm. People might even notice that you're exuding a certain glow from within. If you're in a relationship, you can teach your partner to do what pleasures you most, and invite the divine into your lovemaking. You'll be amazed by the magical flow that occurs as you honor the God and Goddess in each other.

Cosmic Mates

The closest star to our Earth, the Sun, and its companion, the Moon, were especially revered by the ancients. They've long been our reliable companions. Our ancestors observed their symbiotic relationship, imagined them to be cosmic mates, and created rituals intended to replicate their passionate bond. Some myths depict the Sun chasing the Moon around the sky as she plays the cosmic coquette to her beloved. Other traditions see the Sun as feminine, pursuing a masculine Moon. One claimed the Sun loved the Moon so much that he died each night so she might live. Ah, such poetic fancies! They speak to us across the ages, mirroring our own desire to love and be loved that deeply.

My favorite of these romantic images comes from the ancient Hindus, who believed that Shiva, the divine masculine Sun, and Shakti, the divine feminine Moon, are always making love behind the scenes—spreading their passion to all of Creation. Theirs is the embrace that all lovers dream of: a never-ending experience of delight. The passion of these cosmic mates is said to be the vital force that keeps us alive. And, say the sages of old, anyone can tune in to their exquisite cosmic bliss and be blessed with peace, vitality, and radiant health.

Even today in Hindu culture, Shiva and Shakti are invoked at marriages. Some attending the lavish, three-day ceremony may be too distracted by the gorgeous decorations, costumes, and sumptuous meals to experience the event's deeper spiritual significance, though. The priest charges the groom as Shiva to bring steadfastness and protection to his mate while the bride as Shakti is asked to bestow strength and comfort on her beloved. Like yang and yin in Chinese philosophy, their complementary energies bring wholeness to the union.

The more primal version of the sacred marriage may be sensed by some in the riotous dancing that follows the feasting. The bride becomes Shakti, with her full breasts and round hips, dancing sensually to the rhythms of drum and sitar. As the music grows louder, her movements quicken. The bridegroom as Shiva then springs forth to join his beloved. His long hair tumbles down his strong, blue back, glistening with sweat. As the dance peaks, they merge and explode in fiery sparks—returning to primordial unity. Light joins with dark, creation with destruction. The world is created anew.

Egyptian Mysteries

In Egyptian cosmology (and other ancient traditions), the Sky and the Earth are the cosmic mates whose love keeps creation alive. Nut is the sky Goddess, her body arching across the Earth from horizon to horizon. Geb, the Earth God, lies beneath her—his erect phallus forming the axis of creation. The lovers are separated by day, but at night, Nut descends under cover of darkness to meet Geb, and fertilizes the Earth. Because Nut is married to the jealous sun god Ra, she can only be with her true love once Ra retires for the night.

The passion of Nut and Geb begat Isis and Osiris, who were also cosmic mates. These twin souls were everything to each other—brother and sister, husband and wife, priest and priestess, and co-rulers of Egypt in pre-dynastic days. They may or may not have existed in reality, but the profound mysteries surrounding these two permeated all of ancient Egyptian culture and spiritual beliefs.

Isis and Osiris were said to have mated within the womb, magnetized by erotic joy. Their enduring myth—one of the few featuring a married couple who are passionately in love with each other—revealed them working together, bringing to their people all the civilized arts, from agriculture and architecture to music and literature. Torn apart by tragedy, this extraordinary union survived even death, bringing hope of resurrection and eternal life to true believers.

Working the Magic of Isis

You can learn a great deal about the mysteries of Isis and sexual magic from reading the novels of Dion Fortune, a British author who was an initiate of the Isis cult. Moon Magic and The Sea Priestess swept me away into another world, reminding me of secrets I somehow knew but had forgotten. I realized how much humanity relies on the power of women to keep life going on the planet—and not just by birthing babies. Our vitalizing, nourishing essence is needed—now more than ever—to restore our world to its original glory and help heal mankind. In The Sea Priestess, Fortune says that what's needed in the private, sexual side of marriage is the dynamic woman, who owns her power and isn't afraid to direct the course of events. It's this feeling of self-confidence, she adds, that the modest woman lacks.

The author was writing in the first half of the twentieth century, a time when women were expected to be submissive to their mates. The "dynamic woman," whether in public or private, was frowned upon. Now we live in a freer age, where we can launch a business, choose whatever partner we like, and be as dynamic as we want to be. Yet many of us still hold back from expressing our true selves, fearing we'll be rejected.

According to several studies, men find self-confidence to be the most attractive quality a woman can possess. They want us to be more forthcoming about our desires and speak our deepest truth. They need us to tell them what we want so they can provide it (men love to provide!). Most of all, they long for us to be the Goddess to them. It's what every man seeks—and when yours finds it in you, he'll worship you forever.

In the next sections, we'll delve more deeply into your personal Moon. Hopefully I've whetted your appetite for all things lunar, and given you courage to express your inner Goddess more fully—or the permission to do so, if you needed it. The willingness to let your inner Goddess shine forth forms the very foundation of a creatively fulfilled and happy life.

PART 3

Moon In Aries

If your Moon is in fiery Aries, you're known for stating what's on your mind. Headstrong and enthusiastic, you don't have time to wait around, and you tend to go after what you want. You might even have a naughty streak. Though you may not necessarily be a "bad girl," your Moon is ruled by impetuous Mars, so you're always up for a little fun. You also love to play games. An Aries Moon friend of mine is a champion poker player—regularly beating the men she plays with!

And that entrepreneurial streak of yours? That's pure Aries, and it can take you on roads that few have traveled. Look at Rihanna—a woman who likes to be in charge. The feisty Aries singer created her own imprint, became the first black face of Dior, and started her own fashion line. She's an original, and she proudly owns it.

Your Lunar Superpower

Your greatest strength is your authenticity—people know that you're for real. You have a certain twinkle in your eye that others find irresistible. Partly it's the tomboy in you. While other girls were having tea parties, you were probably roughhousing with the boys. Now, you're out pumping iron, running a company, or dancing the night away. You're still very much a woman, but your fierce independence gives you a confidence and capability that few women possess. Also, you're quite resilient. When you get knocked down, you get right back up and keep on fighting.

Your Lunar Shadow

Impatience is your greatest weakness. Have you ever wondered why the moment things get boring or frustrating, you're itching to bolt? It's your Aries Moon impulsiveness; you have a hard time sitting still, and tend to act or speak before you think. You've probably learned how to control this to some extent. Still, people could be shocked when it rears its head. The same goes for your temper. It can blaze up out of nowhere and blow over just as fast. You like to stand up for yourself and confront issues in the moment, but some may have a hard time with your directness—especially the sensitive water signs (Cancer, Scorpio, Pisces). With them, a little diplomacy goes a long way.

Your Sexual Nature

You know instinctively that your libido is an emanation of your Goddess power, and you aren't afraid to ask for what—or who—you desire. Some might say you approach sex the way a man does. Whether it's asking someone out, being willing to try new things in bed, or exposing your feelings early on, your partner always knows where you stand. You prefer to be dominant, or at least equal in calling the shots in bed. Your inner Goddess needs her alone time, however, and your partner must respect that. When younger, you tend to go for excitement over stability. You may have lots of crushes and intense, short-lived relationships. If someone doesn't treat you right, they're apt to get a swift kick out the door. Sparks fly when you connect with other fiery Moon signs (other Aries, Leo, and Sagittarius), though power struggles can also ensue. Air sign Moons (Gemini, Libra, Aquarius) are a great match for you, as they provide perspective. And, you get them out of their heads and into their bodies!

Your Karmic Path

You have an eternally youthful soul—and you bring fresh, vibrant enthusiasm to all you do. In past lives, you learned to rely on yourself and became accustomed to being on your own. Perhaps you were a fierce warrior who fought to defend the tribe. Or, you may have been a top surgeon or other professional who had no time for anything but your work. Either way, it's likely you sacrificed the happiness an intimate relationship can bring. Now you're learning give and take in relating with others. Listen carefully to those you love and do your best to give them what they need. Libra types (Sun, Moon, or Ascendant) can teach you a lot about cultivating balance and harmony in relationships.

Aries Moon Women

Of all the Moon signs, yours is the best at making it in a "man's world." You know your own mind and are self-directed. Being told what to do does not please you. You've no doubt had your share of run-ins with authorities. But your independent streak can also prompt you to become your own boss. In fact, you'd make a great CEO. Even when you work for others, you often choose start-ups or positions in which you can do your own thing and help shape outcomes. You're not big on nine-to-five, although you will work hard to get things done.

Be aware, though, that people may perceive you as so self-sufficient that you don't really need them—or so capable that they can slack off and let you do most of the work. Learning to delegate is an important lesson for you. So is making plenty of time for play, whether with others or alone.

Whether it's adventuring in a new city, going to see a movie, or taking a long walk to be with your thoughts, you enjoy your own company. All the Aries Moon women I know love to travel; they crave getting away and seeing new sights, and they don't mind going on their own. Though you need companionship from time to time, you'd rather be alone than with people you don't find stimulating.

Emotionally, you're pretty resilient. You sometimes take things personally but can get over it quickly, and when you feel bad you usually snap right out of it. And you don't dally when you need to move on. An Aries Moon friend once confided that she never understood why people stay stuck in some life choice that they can change. She said she would never put up with something or someone that wasn't right for her.

ARIES MOON QUALITIES

Impetuous

Pioneering

Youthful

Self-focused

Risk-taking

Hot-tempered

Entrepreneurial

Reckless

Playful

Active

Impatient

Determined

Candid

Many Aries Moon women feel a strong, intimate connection to Luna, especially when she's full. Perhaps that's true for you too. One perceives the Moon as her good, wise friend and deep love companion. Another imagines she has a secret romance with Luna; feeling the moonlight dancing within puts her into a magical, sensual state. A third confided that when she sees the light of the Full Moon she wants to eat it. She literally opens her mouth and sticks out her tongue to try to get some moonlight inside her!

Ancient Aries Moon Goddess: *Hippolyta*

Hippolyta, whose name means "unbridled mare," was the Queen of the Amazons, a legendary tribe of women warriors. According to Greek myth, she was the daughter of Aries, god of war. In an area that's now part of Turkey, the Amazons formed an independent society under Hippolyta.

Imagine the terrifying battle cries of warrior women on horseback, laying their enemies to waste. The ancients claimed that Amazons were the first to tame horses. And we've all heard the legend that Amazons removed their right breast to more easily wield a bow or spear. Yet ancient artwork shows no evidence of it.

The legend of the Amazon Warrior has captivated everyone from Shakespeare, who featured Queen Hippolyta in A Midsummer Night's Dream, to the Amazon-inspired Xena: Warrior Princess and Wonder Woman.

Hippolyta possessed a magic girdle, or fancy leather belt, which was the source of her power and right to rule. Demigod Hercules was sent to obtain this girdle, according to legend. Either he tricked her out of it or she fell in love with him and gave it away willingly—the myths vary. Without it, she lost her autonomy, a frightening thing for an Amazon (or an Aries!). Yet sometimes that's the only way to learn about relatedness.

When in love, even the strongest of us tend to give away our power. Perhaps this is why so many Aires Moon women live alone, for fear of losing their independence. If you've lost your freedom

Hippolyta's Sacred Animal: The Mare

Do you love to ride? Many Aries Moon women do. Flying while atop a galloping horse can give you a sense of freedom. Mares take particularly good care of their riders and respond intuitively to your every thought and move. It's not hard to see why the Amazons bonded deeply with their mares.

Sabine Purps, a German-born dentist with a spirited Aries Moon, has a special relationship with her mare, Abby. Yet at first Sabine was intimidated—and the horse took advantage of it. "She did whatever she wanted to do," says Sabine, who resorted to a lot of butt-pushing and mane-pulling. Finally she realized that Abby was just mirroring her own stubbornness.

Sabine started spending more time grooming and talking to her mare. Soon Abby realized that Sabine was serious about the relationship and began showing affection to her. After that, riding became more than just a fun pastime; it turned into something therapeutic, helping Sabine understand and deal with her impulsive, sometimes willful Aries Moon.

Going horseback riding when the Moon is in Aries can reconnect you with your free spirit as well as teach you valuable lessons about yourself. If riding isn't possible, though, you can also call on your spirit mare to help rejuvenate you. Horses have always been associated with journeys—whether in the inner or outer world. They bring us energy and speed, and they connect us to the power of the land.

If you have a small statue of a horse (a child's toy will do), why not bury it near a favorite tree and ask for Hippolyta's blessing with whatever lies ahead for you? Just dig a small hole and reverently bury the statue, while imagining yourself galloping away into a new phase of your life.

---

or have walled yourself off from intimate relationships, light a red candle to Hippolyta and affirm your strength and autonomy—balanced with healthy relatedness. Do this when the Moon is in Aries if you can.

If you have an Aries Moon, you probably possess more energy and stamina than most—yet you're still at risk for burnout. If you're working too much, your warrior may need a time-out.

That's what Dublin-born Siobhán Wilcox, a spiritual life coach, realized when she suffered burnout at twenty-four. She'd been working seven days a week for twelve hours at a stretch. Now she sees the burnout as a blessing that forced her to take care of herself. Though she's still driven, she now takes plenty of breaks. And she's on better terms than ever with her inner warrior.

"My alter ego is a Viking," Siobhán admits. "I'm very fierce—and when my Viking comes out, people flee!"

Creating an Altar to Hippolyta

There are times in life when we all need extra strength and fortitude. No matter your Moon sign, creating an altar to honor Hippolyta will help bring out your inner Amazon.

You Will Need:

- 1 red candle
- 1 knife or sword
- 1 picture of yourself at your most powerful
- 1 picture of Hippolyta, Xena, or Wonder Woman
- 1 tooled leather belt, if you have one
- 1 piece of garnet, obsidian, or a gold nugget
- 1 stick of sage
- 1 picture or statue of a mare
- anything else that says "power and autonomy" to you
- 1 lighter

Making an altar is simple and fun. First, collect the objects listed at left, or any others that light your Aries fire. Then find a spot in your home that instinctively feels right. Perhaps it's the mantle over your fireplace or a small table tucked away in a corner of your bedroom. If it's the latter, you may wish to drape a reddish cloth over the table (Aries is associated with the color red). Then place the items you've gathered on top of it, in a pattern that feels good to you. Take some time with this; you may want to move things around until the altar "clicks." You'll feel it when this happens. Then light the sage and blow the sacred smoke onto your creation to bless and consecrate it.

This can be a temporary altar for the New or Full Moon in Aries, or a more permanent one if you need ongoing courage during a challenging period of your life. You can work with this altar in conjunction with the Moon rituals in this chapter, or any time you need more strength and energy. You might want to light the candles each morning to thank Hippolyta for awakening your Amazon spirit. If you've had your natal chart interpreted and know where Aries falls for you, you could call on Hippolyta's help for strength and drive in that area of life.

The Moon rituals at the end of this chapter will provide further suggestions on how to work with your new Amazon altar. Meanwhile, you can consecrate it by lighting the red candle and asking Hippolyta to give you strength and courage. If you know where Aries is contained within your chart, focus on strengthening that area in particular.

New Moon Ritual:
Breath of Fire

Sometimes because of the daily grind or pushing too hard for too long, your inner fire sputters out. If you've been working a lot or under a great deal of stress, the following ritual will get your flame burning brightly again. It will also help channel and balance your inner fire, especially if Aries is your Moon sign. You might even enjoy this practice so much that you'll want to make it a daily habit.

You can focus on whatever you like, but it's best to choose something for you as an individual. Don't fear being "selfish"—Aries is all about making yourself happy. Your intention might be, "I'm brave enough to ask for a raise and get it." Or, "My body is completely healthy and whole."

Because the dark of the Moon is a seed-planting time, you'll be turning inward. Known as Breath of Fire, the following practice will magnetically recharge your entire body, bringing new life to your tired cells and amplifying your intention. Look for results within two weeks at the Full Moon, which often brings New Moon intentions to fruition.

Make sure you're in reasonably good health before attempting this, as the breathing can get intense. If you feel light-headed, stop and rest. Taking good care of yourself is paramount!

You Will Need:

- a quiet place
- an intention
- your Hippolyta altar or just a red candle
- 1 smudge stick of sage, an abalone shell or a bowl, and matches
- your journal and a pen

1. First, light your red candle (on your altar to Hippolyta if you've created one, or in any secure place). Then light your sage stick and cleanse your aura by passing the smoke up and down your body, as you imagine any tiredness or negativity wafting away. Give it all up to Hippolyta and let her carry it away. Stub the smudge stick out in your shell or bowl.

2. Find a quiet, comfortable spot to sit and focus on your intention. Take some slow, deep breaths to relax and center yourself. Feel your intention in your body as if it were already a reality. Conjure an image of yourself asking for that raise and getting it, or visualize feeling healthy, rejuvenated, and restored, or whatever image suits the goal you are working on.

3. Take three long, slow breaths from the base of your belly. After your third inhalation, rapidly exhale from your nose while forcing the air out and powerfully contracting your belly inward. Repeat, aiming for around two to three breaths per second. If you've never done this before, you may need to practice a bit. It should feel as if your belly is pumping like a bellows. Soon you'll feel a rhythm take over, and your breathing will be fairly effortless. You may enter a trance-like state, in which the outer world disappears. Keep focusing on your intention. Be aware of what you're feeling and sensing.

4. Continue this breathing for five to ten minutes, unless you start to feel faint and need a break. Especially if you're new to this, do no more than five minutes the first time. You can work up to ten minutes as you practice. Once you feel complete, shift back into long, deep, easy breathing and sit quietly as you feel the life-giving energies pulsing through you.

5. Give thanks to Hippolyta for filling you with her magic, and trust that she'll help you manifest your intention in perfect timing. Blow out the candle, and write down any insights in your journal. If you received intuitive instructions (perhaps someone to call or a medicinal herb to research), carry them out quickly. New Moon magic only works if you work it!

Full Moon Ritual:
Give and Take

The Aries Full Moon occurs while the Sun is in Libra, sign of relationships, and the Moon is in Aries, sign of the individual. There's an inherent tension between these two signs, since they're at opposite ends of a polarity, but they also balance each other out. It's hard to have a fulfilling relationship (Libra) unless you know yourself (Aries) well enough to choose the right person—and hold your boundaries. And it's hard to enjoy being footloose (Aries) for very long unless you have close relationships (Libra) you can count on.

We'll be exploring the balance between freedom and closeness, giving and receiving. But first it's good to ask yourself: Do you instinctively pull back when others come close? Or perhaps you let others in too quickly and end up feeling drained? You may have internal shields you're not aware of; this ritual will help you get in touch with them. It's adapted from a process created by Devra Gregory, high priestess of our Dragon Sister Circle.

Stay silent throughout the ritual; you'll be discussing it at the end. Take as long as you need with each part; certain phases of the process may take longer than others, if you sense that you or your partner need more time. Be open to feelings that may well up. This ritual can trigger deep memories along with tears.

You Will Need:

- a friend or partner
- a private place that feels safe and secure
- your Hippolyta altar, if you've made one
- 1 sage stick, an abalone shell or bowl, and matches
- your journal and a pen

1. If you're doing this at home, light your red candle on your Hippolyta altar and ask her to bless the ritual.

2. Face your partner and take three deep breaths while looking into each other's eyes. Then bow to each other with hands in Namaste (prayer position at the heart), to salute the Goddess within each of you.

3. Light the sage and take turns smudging each other: Slowly move the smoke up and down each other's bodies in front and back. Let all cares waft away with the smoke. Then stub the sage out in your shell or bowl.

4. Hug each other for at least thirty seconds, your heart against hers. Breathe slowly. Put up invisible barriers against your partner and shut down your heart, while she gives you love from her open heart. How does this feel?

5. Repeat the process, but in this case both of you will focus on shutting down your hearts and putting up invisible shields as you hug. Does that feel any different?

6. Now switch roles. While focused on giving from your heart, hug your partner for at least ten seconds, while she puts up barriers and shuts down her heart. How does that feel?

7. Repeat the process, still focused on giving, but this time your partner opens her heart and lets herself receive. This part of the ritual should feel incredibly expansive. Can you sense the difference when you hug her this time?

8. When you feel complete, salute each other again with Namaste.

9. Now sit down and take turns sharing with each other. What came up for you? Did you have any significant insights? How was it to shut down and deliberately not give of yourself? What about opening up? Was it easy or hard to let the other person in? Did you feel safe? Perhaps you became aware of a tendency to over-give, or to push people away. Share any vulnerabilities or strengths you became aware of, and listen closely as your partner does the same. This experience can be very bonding!

10. When you're done, blow out the candle and write in your journal about your insights.

When The Moon Is In Aries

Each month the Moon spends two-and-a-half days in the joyful sign of Aries. This is when your childlike enthusiasm can take you far. No matter your Moon sign, you should feel more upbeat and energetic, and you'll have the ability to get a lot done. Because you'll also be feeling braver than usual, it's a good time to take on new projects and advance your career. But it's also easy to exhaust yourself trying to do too much, staying up too late working or partying, or burning the candle at both ends.

The key to accomplishing things under an Aries Moon is to pace yourself. Work hard in spurts and then take a break to do some stretches or meet a friend for lunch. Keep things fun, maybe by playing your favorite music as you work, so you're less likely to lose interest in the task at hand. Avoid powering through if you get bored or frustrated. Take a few minutes to close your eyes and regenerate your energy, then return to the task. If you still have excess energy or frustrations by the day's end, put them to good use by attacking that dirty floor or going for a run.

Make sure you get a good workout in, as you'll need to channel any excess fire during this cycle. It's easy to get impulsive or impatient with yourself or others during this Moon cycle (especially if Aries is your Moon sign). Tempers can flare, so think before you speak.

Aries is an on-the-go sign, which makes this a great time to travel. Even if you just visit a different neighborhood, delight your senses with fresh sights and sounds. As the first sign of the zodiac, Aries loves whatever is unique and original.

THINGS TO DO WHEN THE MOON IS IN ARIES

Initiate a new project

Make career-related calls

Work out or go on a hike

Buy new sports equipment

Do a fire ceremony to let go of the past

Take a trip—even if it's just across town

Play with kids and let your inner child out

Go horseback riding or take a martial arts class

Build a campfire

Go to an amusement park and drive bumper cars!

Play loud music and dance out your joy or frustrations`

PART 4

Moon in Taurus

The ancients knew there was no separation between themselves and Mama Earth. They sensed that nature's sacred flora and fauna have the power to awaken the soul. You know this, too, if your Moon is in earthy Taurus. Your connection to nature is so strong that the Moon is said to be "exalted," or at her best, in this fertile sign. And because Taurus is ruled by sensuous Venus, you're also deeply feminine.

In our busy world, it's easy to lose touch with nature. Fortunately, if you have Moon in Taurus, you hear the Earth's call. Your Moon will gently but persistently remind you to engage with the natural world. In an idle moment, you'll glance out a window and see a bird or a butterfly beckoning you to breathe and reconnect.

Your Lunar Superpower

If you were born with Moon in Taurus, your superpower is your steadfast devotion. Have you ever wondered why others turn to you for guidance and a shoulder to lean on? It's the calming, grounding effect of your Moon. It lights a path for those who are in darkness, leading them into the light. Just be sure to support others to find their own way instead of always doing things for them.

Being so earthy, you love the material world. You appreciate nice things, and usually make enough money to afford them. You like to be surrounded by beauty, and your home usually contains many artful elements. You love to cook (or cater) a yummy meal for friends or family. Sitting down to a sumptuous feast with those you love is your Moon sign's idea of heaven.

Your Lunar Shadow

Overindulgence is your weakness. Your sensual nature is so strong that it can lead you down a treacherous path when it comes to sex and/or food. Gratifying the urges of the flesh is healthy to a point, but your Moon doesn't always know when that point has been crossed. Gardening or hiking in nature can fill you up in other ways.

Your passion for the material world can also lead to overspending. Taurus Moon often seeks security through possessing things. Being unwilling to say no could lead to trouble, such as a wardrobe of expensive clothes you rarely wear. Though most Taurus Moons are scrupulously honest, expensive tastes can, in some cases, lead to credit card debt or cheating on taxes.

Your Sexual Nature

The most sensual sign of all, Taurus craves physical pleasure. Your idea of heaven is to spend all day in bed with your lover, exploring each other's bodies and savoring sexual delights. Whoever came up with the idea of licking whipped cream off someone's body probably had a Taurus Moon. Long, slow, and deep is how you like it. Teach your mate how to pamper and adore the Goddess in you.

Your sex drive is strong, but you're patient and will wait until the moment and setting are right. Security is your aphrodisiac, so you need someone who's going to stick around. You're in it for the long haul once you find the right person. As long as you're comfortable, making love outdoors can be a turn-on. The earthy Moon signs (Taurus, Virgo, and Capricorn) satisfy your need for leisurely sex and enduring devotion. The watery Moons (Cancer, Scorpio, and Pisces) touch your emotions and soul, while you give them the stability they crave.

Your Karmic Path

You have the soul of a nature Goddess. But in previous lives, you learned to value comfort and security. Perhaps you didn't venture far from the family farm, or remained in a job that paid the bills rather than finding something more fulfilling. You may also have relied too much on material things to make you happy. In this life, you're learning to share. You need to find security in the intangibles of life, such as inner peace and time with loved ones, rather than a plump bank account or the biggest house on the block. Being of use to others is what will make you happy now, as long as you don't overdo it. Being in nature will remind you who you are—and have always been.

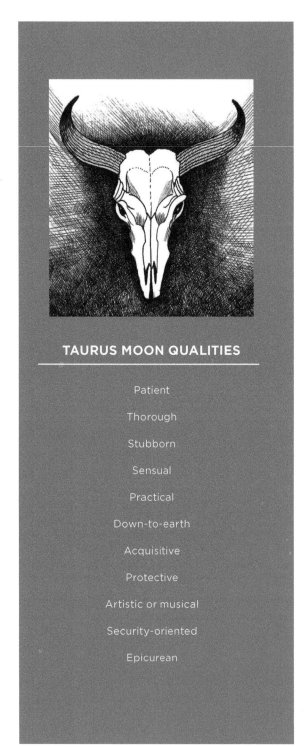

TAURUS MOON QUALITIES

Patient

Thorough

Stubborn

Sensual

Practical

Down-to-earth

Acquisitive

Protective

Artistic or musical

Security-oriented

Epicurean

Taurus Moon Women

Sweet and charming yet tough as nails, the Taurus Moon woman gets things done. You have a sultry yet steely charm that draws others in. People trust you. They often count on your stability and dependability to stabilize their lives. For better or for worse, you are their rock.

Like prolific Taurus author Jean Houston, still going strong in her twilight years, you have endurance and commitment. Houston travels the world teaching people how to awaken their full potential. She is a force of nature who works eighteen-hour days. Yet, as she confided to us in her July 2015 Awakening To Your Life's Purpose teleseminar, she still finds time to cook her Sicilian mother's delectable dishes for friends. Her philosophy is practical and down to earth, said Houston: She simply tries to be of use.

Because you're such a trooper, though, it's easy to overextend your energies. When she hits the wall, a hard-working Taurus Moon massage therapist friend goes out and plants her feet on the grass, takes a few deep breaths, and pours her tensions into the Earth. Don't be afraid to give your frustrations to your Earth Mama—she can take it! Like my friend, you'll return to work with renewed energy.

If you stay away too long from your Earth Mama, daily concerns will consume and exhaust you. Neglecting the sensual side of your nature is asking for trouble.

Sometimes you have trouble falling asleep at night, or toss and turn while trying to solve problems in your sleep. Avoid working or watching the news right before sleep. Regular massage is essential, especially if you suffer from sleep deprivation. An insomniac pal of mine with Taurus Moon found deep rest in a sensory deprivation tank. After ninety minutes of floating in total silence, she said she felt like she'd had a six-hour massage. She had returned to the womb and been reborn.

Crystals and gemstones can be a source of replenishment too. One Taurus Moon friend makes healing gemstone jewelry, which centers and uplifts her. There's something about working quietly with your hands that Taurus Moons find deeply satisfying. You may love needlepoint or sewing. You can also find your flow while pruning a rose bush. You may be communing with plant devas without even knowing it!

Because Taurus rules the throat and voice, you probably love to hum along with songs or sing in the shower. Using your voice can be deeply freeing. You may also find fulfillment by joining a chorus or doing karaoke.

Home is your sanctuary and you need to feel absolutely comfortable there. However, many Taurus Moons stay too long in one place, collecting a lot of stuff and then feeling trapped by it. If this is you, clutter-clearing can be the best therapy of all.

Lakshmi's Sacred Animal: The Elephant

Taurus has long been associated with the fertile bull; in ancient times the bull's horns equated to the crescent Moon. To me, however, the elephant captures the steadfast feminine spirit of Taurus even better. Elephant societies are matriarchal. They maintain close social networks and share resources with their extended family. Herds are led by the wisest and oldest female, who remembers where water holes, food sources, and danger zones lie. Like the bull, the elephant's power comes not from speed, but Taurean endurance and street smarts.

The fact that elephants are often coupled with Lakshmi tells us that the strength, devotion, and keen instincts of the elephant are keys to living an abundant and happy life. Widely revered as the remover of obstacles, the elephant god Ganesha is worshipped throughout India, and increasingly, the West.

Near the difficult end of my father's life, a Vedic (Indian) astrologer advised me to do a forty-day puja, or prayer ritual, to Ganesha. My chants and offerings to the elephant god helped Dad transition peacefully and enabled me to move on. Ganesha will help you overcome any obstacle you're facing if you leave a small offering of yogurt or fruit for him when the Moon is in Taurus. Do this at the altar you'll be creating.

Your ritual doesn't have to be complicated; just ask for Ganesha's help as you leave your offering. If you know where Taurus falls in your chart, ask him to bless that part of your life. Also, giving a donation in Ganesha's name to help rescue elephants being mistreated in zoos, circuses, and temples worldwide is sure to garner his assistance.

Ancient Taurus Moon Goddess: *Lakshmi*

Radiating the sensual power of the Taurus Moon, the Hindu goddess Lakshmi sits on a lotus wearing a beautiful pink sari, with coins spilling out of her hands. Like the lotus, she arose from the sacred mud of the Earth to bless us with its riches and beauty. Lakshmi reminds us how life should be lived—in pleasure and abundance. Revered by Hindus as the Mother of the Earth, her freely given coins represent her compassion and charity for all living creatures.

Lakshmi's sensual relationship with her husband Lord Vishnu is depicted in temple carvings throughout India, sometimes with Lakshmi leaning against Vishnu's chest as he tenderly cups her breast in his palm. Lakshmi is also associated with the stalwart, Taurean elephant. Hindus worship her along with the elephant god Ganesha each autumn at Diwali, the festival of lights. The faithful don their most beautiful clothing, light candles, and then invoke Lord Ganesha to remove all obstacles to wealth, after which Lakshmi is invited to rain down her blessings.

It may be easiest to invoke Lakshmi when the Moon is in Taurus, but like any true Goddess, she's always available. I have a wall hanging of her above my morning altar, and I call her name each day. As a beautiful representative of the Taurus energy, she brings us greater abundance of all kinds, from money to love to inner peace. Be sure to call on her (preferably at the Lakshmi altar you'll be making) before a job interview or asking for a raise, or prior to making love to a partner for the first time. Leave a few coins to remind her of your gratitude for her gifts.

Creating an Altar to Lakshmi

An altar that invites Lakshmi's presence should reflect both earthly and heavenly delights because she is the most sensual and yet spiritual of Goddesses.

You Will Need:

- 1 belly dance sash, ideally one with coins on it
- 1 image or statue of Lakshmi and Ganesha
- fragrant flowers and incense
- 1 bowl of coins or wad of cash
- jeweled necklaces or other adornments
- red, purple, or green candles
- 1 bowl of fruit

Drape a belly dance sash or a luxurious piece of jewel-toned fabric over a table, and place your images of Lakshmi and/or Ganesha in the center. Assemble beautiful objects, colors, jewels, flowers, candles, and other offerings to please your eye as well as your soul. Now you're set to worship not only Lakshmi and Ganesha, but the Goddess within you.

Taurus is a sensuous energy, and this altar is intended to stimulate your senses. One of the easiest ways to awaken your inner Goddess is through smelling heavenly scents, tasting luscious flavors, and wearing gorgeous clothing. When the Moon is in Taurus, light incense or scented candles on your altar to bless the day—and blow Lakshmi and Ganesha a kiss. Wear the beautiful necklace you'd left on the altar, tuck one of the flowers behind your ear, or take a bite of the ripe fruit. Then go forth into the world, knowing that good fortune will bless your day.

New Moon Ritual:
Green Magic

The following ritual is designed to help you reconnect with the abundant, green power of nature.

I'm grateful to Siobhán Wilcox for letting me use her process of communing with plants. She says that plants and trees are part of fifth-dimensional, or "oneness" consciousness. This is the state of being—connected, tuned in, optimally healthy—that will help us thrive and ensure the survival of our species. In communing with the plant world, we open our hearts to receive a transfusion of green energy and to access oneness consciousness so we can heal ourselves and the world.

I enhanced this ritual by adding cash. How, you might wonder, are plants and cash related? They're both green energy. Money can be part of oneness consciousness if you approach it with reverence. It's meant to flow in and out of your life, bringing abundance and well-being. As an exchange for your purposeful work, money is sacred, an acknowledgment from the universe that you're on the right track with your contribution. Money allows you to care for yourself and others.

This ritual will help banish any negative associations around money, your value, or your ability to receive what you deserve. It will help you shake off any old programming still lurking in your subconscious mind, such as "money is dirty" or "there is never enough." money to go around." Take at least an hour for this ritual, with no pressing engagements afterward.

You Will Need:

- your Lakshmi altar and/or a green candle
- 1 healthy green plant with substantial leaves (a jade plant is ideal)
- as much cash as possible; large bills are great
- your journal and a pen

1. Light the green candle on your altar and ask Lakshmi and Ganesha to bless your ritual. Then sit at a table, indoors or outdoors, with your plant in front of you. Place your pile of cash and your journal and pen beside you.

2. Sit with your plant and breathe deeply to ground yourself. Imagine the Earth Mama's energy coming up from the center of the Earth through the bottoms of your feet. As you breathe in, pull it all the way up to the crown of your head. As you breathe out, send it back down through your feet into the Earth. Do this at least three times, until you feel calm and centered.

3. Place your right hand on your heart, and gently hold a leaf of the plant with your left hand. Feel a sense of gratitude in your heart. Tell the plant how much you appreciate it, how wise and beautiful it is. If you feel silly or uncomfortable, just breathe through it. Your plant is a living being that loves appreciation, just like you do. Although it vibrates at a different level of consciousness, it can sense what you need and it wants to help. Ask the plant to send you some of its green juice. Soon you'll start to feel a slight buzzing or throbbing sensation in your fingers, as the plant responds. Open yourself to fully receive the gift. Ask if there is anything you need to know to gain greater prosperity and well-being. The message may come as an image, an impulse, a word or phrase, or a feeling.

4. Once you're brimming with green juice, thank the plant and lay your hands in your lap. Breathe quietly and stay attuned to your heart. Then take your pile of cash and spread it around the plant. Infuse the green energy into the money as you slowly move your hands back and forth over it. Say the following: "Sacred cash, I hereby command that with each wave of my hand, you take on increased power and energy, and bring great prosperity back to me." Then radiate appreciation to the money, just as you did to the plant. When you feel complete, put the super-charged cash in your wallet. Know that each time you spend it, your prosperity will grow. Avoid spending it all at once, though—patient Taurus prefers you find just the right things to use it for.

5. Return to your altar and give thanks to Lakshmi as you blow out the candle. Then note in your journal any "ah-has" or "must-dos" that came to you, especially any positive thoughts that could become your new power statement (such as, "Money comes easily to me and I spend it wisely" or "I am one with money and it treats me well.") Then go forth with your new prosperity consciousness!

Full Moon Ritual:
Walking the Labyrinth

A labyrinth is an intuitive tool that helps us quiet the mind and get centered. It's like a walking prayer. Your labyrinth can be built of stones, marbles, chalk, or whatever you choose. Nowadays the spiral design is even printed on a portable tarp you can roll out and put away later. A labyrinth is not the same as a maze, in which you can get lost. The labyrinth has only one path to the center and back.

The labyrinth's mandala-like configuration dates from ancient times and can be found in cathedrals (most famously, the Chartres Cathedral in France), as well as retreat settings. Check your area for a church or spiritual group that does labyrinth walks, or create one yourself, like I did. Ever since my friends and I created a river rock labyrinth in my backyard, I've walked it each morning to bless the day.

You Will Need:

- your Lakshmi altar and a green candle
- access to a labyrinth, or stones to create your own
- comfortable walking shoes
- an intention
- like-minded friends, if you choose
- your journal and a pen

The Taurus Full Moon occurs when the Sun is in Scorpio. Known as the Wesak Festival, this is one of the strongest Full Moons of the year. With earthy, stable Taurus opposite watery, deep-feeling Scorpio, magic is definitely afoot! If you can do this ritual outdoors at night, you'll be able to feel the Full Moon's power in its fullest intensity.

1. Light the green candle on your altar and share your intention with Lakshmi. Perhaps it's for healing, a deeper connection with yourself, or greater prosperity. Then if you're creating a labyrinth, set your center stone and slowly begin placing the other stones into a simple spiral formation radiating out from that. Make the path wide enough to comfortably walk. You may need to reposition the stones as you go. If you're using a portable labyrinth or walking an existing one, go on to the next step.

2. Go outside if you're not already there, and raise your arms to the Moon. Say, "Hail and welcome, Lakshmi!" Stand at the opening of the labyrinth and focus on your intention. Breathe the Earth Mama's energy into your body from the bottom of your feet to the top of your head. Then step inside and begin walking slowly, with awareness. Release any fears or concerns as you walk; the journey to the center is about letting go. You may shed tears; this is perfectly natural, as the Full Moon stimulates our emotions.

3. When you reach the center, stay as long as you like. Receive whatever gifts or answers are waiting for you. People sometimes have spiritual experiences here; be open to whatever wants to

come, even if it's merely a sense of well-being or connectedness.

4. As you follow the return path, absorb what you've received. Breathe deeply as you feel gratitude for Mama Earth's support and your renewed clarity or sense of purpose. At the end, raise your arms and draw Luna's power into your body, saying, "Hail and farewell, Lakshmi!" Blow out the candle on your altar. Then share with your friends and/or write in your journal about the experience.

time for a grueling workout—a leisurely walk or yoga class is more Taurus's speed. Take a nap, get a massage, or trade shoulder rubs with a friend. You might enjoy doing an art project such as collage or coloring, or buying flowers to beautify your home (including your altar to Lakshmi). Taurus Moon is a wonderful time for lovemaking, so schedule some quality time with your beloved—or your own sensual self. Enjoy the exquisite power of touch and the slow, pleasurable exchange of loving energies.

When The Moon Is In Taurus

The pace of life has accelerated to the point that most of us feel overwhelmed and behind schedule. Luckily, the time of the month when the Moon is in Taurus helps us slow down long enough to counteract that trend. Taurus wants us to focus on our bodies and savor life fully. This Moon Goddess is in the here-and-now. Start by preparing a delicious breakfast, and really take your time chewing and tasting it. Feel the nutrients feeding every cell and sense your body's deep appreciation for the nourishment.

Move mindfully through your daily routine, from washing the dishes to getting dressed and interacting with others. That's how you access the pleasure of life—by being present in each moment. You can get a lot done when the Moon is in earthy Taurus, which favors work and making money.

If the Taurus Moon has you feeling a bit lazy, indulge that feeling. This is probably not the best

THINGS TO DO WHEN THE MOON IS IN TAURUS

Clean and beautify your home

Ask for a raise or look for more rewarding work

Spend time on a creative or money-making project

Deepen your sensual connection to someone you love

Plant a garden or prune plants

Put a one hundred dollar bill in your wallet to feel wealthy

Get a luxurious beauty treatment

Lie or walk barefoot on the grass

Buy beautiful gifts for others

Go to a belly-dancing or yoga class

Make a delicious meal

Balance your checkbook

PART 5

Moon in Gemini

If your Moon is in inquisitive Gemini, figuring things out is comforting to you. Your mind is always active, whether studying, writing, gathering data, or discussing who said what and why. It often keeps you awake at night, rehashing the day's events.

Meditation was invented for people like you, but will you sit still long enough to do it? Try yoga. Air sign Moons, especially Geminis, need to get out of their heads and into their bodies.

It's not that you lack feelings if you have Moon in Gemini. It's just that you learned early on to get by on your wits. Analyzing and talking about your feelings may be easy, but actually letting yourself experience them could take some practice.

Your Lunar Superpower

Your greatest strength is your keen perception. You hear, see, and feel things more acutely than most people do. You don't miss a trick. When the world speaks to you, you pay attention. That's what makes you such a great writer and speaker—your powers of observation and ability to translate what you perceive in ways others can understand.

Most Gemini Moons learn to read early on and love escaping into a good book. Perhaps your mother read to you, sparking your lifelong love of learning. Yet your childhood had its ups and downs. Maybe your family moved around a lot, which made you feel insecure. But you learned that the only constant is change, and you received good training in remaining flexible.

Your Lunar Shadow

Aloofness is your downfall. Because it's so easy to distance yourself from your feelings, you could be seen as above-it-all or even uncaring. But that's usually the furthest thing from the truth. It's just easier to shut down and pretend you're not affected by things.

Although your active imagination is a great asset, it can also work against you, conjuring frights out of thin air. As they say, don't believe everything you think. The next time you experience a thought attack, repeat this mantra from Zen master Sono: "Thank you for everything. I have no complaint whatsoever." It brings detachment and calmness.

Your Sexual Nature

Sex happens in your mind as much as in your body. You need to communicate your feelings and ask for what you want in order to be fully engaged. Otherwise you're apt to drift off into fantasies. In or out of bed, you'll keep your mate entertained with your wry observations. Though you love to bond, you also need a bit of breathing room—so a lover who's too clingy or demanding would never work for you. You need a lot of stimulation and love to try new things. What you desire one day might be different the next. Keep your partner in the loop so he can flow with your changing needs. The air sign Moons (Gemini, Libra, and Aquarius) are good for you, with their quick wit, charm, and flexibility. You'd also do well with fiery Moons (Aries, Leo, Sagittarius) who share your sense of adventure, although you may find them too controlling.

Your Karmic Path

You have the soul of a seeker. In past lives, you dipped in and out of so many studies and/or occupations that you never managed to master any of them. You may still be a bit of a dilettante (though now we might call you a multitasker!), but you're learning to not spread yourself too thin. In this life, you're challenged to pick one thing, go into it deeply, and stick with it—whether it's a career, relationship, or spiritual path.

Discipline is the best medicine for you. This particularly applies to your connection to the physical world (being in your body, creating financial or internal stability). Don't let the word *discipline* scare you, though. It just means being a disciple to yourself, and loving yourself so much that you're willing to do those workouts or save that money—or make that long-term commitment. This lifetime is not about scrambling to manage a million details—staying focused on the big picture will reward you.

Gemini Moon Women

Gemini Moon women tend to find each other. That cool woman you always chat with at the gym? Probably a Gemini Moon (or Ascendant). Many of my closest friends are Gemini types. We speak the same language, and we easily make each other laugh.

Although you're quite social, you're not always a party girl. Because Gemini is symbolized by the Twins, you have two distinct sides. When you're up, you're on top of the world. But then you come crashing down and need to withdraw and shut people out. If you stay too long on the dark side of your Moon, however, you run the risk of getting stuck. When that happens, try putting on some tribal music and dancing out the dark mood. Writing in your journal can also help.

If your Moon is in heady Gemini, cultivating more pleasure is crucial. Because you're such a busy bee, having "slow days," when you unplug the phone and putter around the house, is great therapy. Scheduling important pleasure dates ahead of time will make sure they happen.

Wouldn't it have been great if our mothers had taught us that pleasure is our birthright? If you have children, you can teach them how to find their own pleasures—and refuse those they don't enjoy.

GEMINI MOON QUALITIES

Smart

Quick-witted

Adaptable

Ingenious

Easily bored

Good writer, speaker

Imaginative

Perceptive

Aloof

Charming

Fun

Affectionate

Fidgety

Irritable

A friend's fifteen-year-old Gemini Moon daughter learned early on how to be her own person. Her mom says she's an old soul, thoughtful in her words and actions, who speaks her mind. No sexting or hooking up for this young woman—she'd rather read Dante! And her mom doesn't worry about her losing her way.

Being able to find your way is a Gemini Moon trait. Your connection to messenger Mercury (Gemini's ruling planet) attunes you to your inner GPS. Your sensitive antennae may even give you psychic abilities. One Gemini Moon woman I know experiences precognitive moments that lead her to key people and information. She'll have a strong urge to go somewhere, but she doesn't know where. So she jumps in the car and drives until she feels she's in the right place. She once ended up at a restaurant she'd never been to before, yet knew exactly where she wanted to sit. And there she found someone she'd been longing to see.

Your active mind finds inspiration while on the move. Gemini Moon writer April Elliott Kent told me her best song lyrics come to her while driving, and she wrote much of her last book on a train, prompted by its steady rhythm. This is worth trying if you have writers' block!

Gemini is an androgynous sign, and tuning into your feminine side can sometimes be tricky. A Gemini Moon pal says she's been practicing her receptive, feminine skills on her diabetic cat. When it comes time for the daily insulin shot, rather than forcing the issue she patiently relaxes and breathes from her belly, "magnetizing" her reluctant kitty out of hiding. And, she reports, it works like a charm.

Scheherazade's Sacred Animal: The Monkey

The ingenious primate, a very social creature, is a perfect totem for the curious, witty Gemini Moon. The monkey also mirrors Scheherazade's intelligence, resourcefulness, and artful trickery. Though the monkey is more of a practical jokester, our sensuous storyteller raised the art of trickery to a higher level.

Like Gemini, however, the monkey has a dual nature. Although they bond intensely with one another and display kindness and caring for their families, primates also have a dark side. They can be erratic, unpredictable, and even vicious, especially when interacting with animals outside their community.

Scheherazade channels her trickster nature more gently. She's so well rooted in her healing instincts that she knows she can trick a damaged man into loving and trusting her—and help him find redemption.

In her book *Women Who Run with the Wolves*, Clarissa Pinkola Estes says that all women have an outer self who lives by the light of day and is easy to see, plus an interior self who dwells in the depths and is harder to understand (especially for men). I'd add that this duality is especially strong in women with Moon in Gemini, because you're ruled by the Twins. Your distinct light and dark sides often keep people guessing.

Finding that balance between inner and outer is the Gemini Moon's task. Inspired by the monkey, you can learn to honor your dual nature— hopefully minus the vicious streak! Monkeys love to play more than anything else, so the secret to staying balanced is to make sure you're getting your quota of play time.

Ancient Gemini Moon Goddess: *Scheherazade*

Scheherazade is one of the most inspiring feminine figures who ever "lived." (It's unclear whether her legend is based in fact.) Because of her extraordinary bravery, cleverness, and storytelling skills, I've appointed her our ancient Gemini Moon Goddess.

In the famous Arabian Nights story, a sultan discovered his wife had been unfaithful to him. Consumed by fury and despair, he refused to ever be betrayed again. So he hatched a sinister plot to marry, bed, and then kill a virgin each day.

When Scheherazade learned of his plans, she volunteered to marry him. No ordinary virgin, this accomplished young woman was well versed in literature and knew all the poets'

works by heart. She'd also loved the sultan since they played together as children. At their marriage, she wore a gown embroidered with plants and animals, befitting her status as a nature Goddess.

That night, Scheherazade began spinning a beguiling tale for her husband. At first he resisted, but the story was so compelling that he spared her life so she might continue it the next night. It took many nights (some versions of the legend say 1,001) to transform the sultan and heal his hardened heart, during which time he grew more and more enraptured with his wife. Scheherazade's brave act taught the sultan how to rise out of darkness and become the wise ruler he was born to be.

If you have Moon in Gemini, you too are capable of spinning grand tales that enrapture and enlighten others. Maybe it's as simple as the funny story you tell a friend that lightens her mood, or the letter to the editor you write that mobilizes your community to resolve an issue. Invoke Scheherazade when the Moon is in Gemini, or any time you need help with communication-related matters. Light a blue candle to her (ideally on the altar you'll be making) prior to a job interview or a first date, and ask her to place the right words in your mouth for the perfect outcome.

Creating an Altar to Scheherazade

Because Scheherazade was a nature Goddess who loved books and learning, you'll want to create an altar that represents both of those elements. You can find wonderful images online representing our lovely Persian goddess—why not print one out and frame it for your altar?

You'll be using this altar in the New and Moon rituals that follow, but you can set it up ahead of time, especially if you have Moon in Gemini and want to deepen your ruling Goddess's magic in your life. Create your altar wherever you like, though it's especially good to have it in your office, library, or TV room—anyplace that communication takes place. Why not dedicate the top of your bookshelf to it?

If you know your astrology chart, you can see where Gemini falls and focus on that area of life. Or, just go on instinct. Preferably when the Moon is in Gemini, set up your altar in a pleasing way and consecrate it by lighting incense and a blue candle. Spend a few moments focusing on Scheherazade and her monkey totem. Thank them for blessing your life. You can also pose a question, write it down, and leave it on the altar. Stay alert for the answer, which is apt to arrive in the next few days.

You Will Need:

- 1 image representing Scheherazade
- a few beautiful, preferably hard-bound books (legends or poetry would be ideal)
- 1 blue or green scarf as a base for the altar
- malachite or lapis stones
- 1 image or figure of a monkey
- 1 green plant or vase of flowers
- some bewitching incense
- 1 blue candle

New Moon Ritual:
A Healing Mantra

Gemini Moon people usually prefer quick, casual rituals; no solemn, formal ceremonies for your get-to-the-point Moon. But you do enjoy pondering deep questions. And you can benefit greatly from adopting a mantra—a simple word or phrase that, when repeated regularly, comforts you and keeps you on track.

The Gemini New Moon is a good time to go deep into the darkness and find the treasures that lie buried there. Chances are, you've learned to devalue the darkness, or even fear it. We all have. We judge ourselves for falling into bad moods or wanting to stay home rather than go out to be with friends. Yet you need periodic visits to the Underworld, especially if you have an air sign Moon. This ritual will help you relax into the darkness, or womb-space—your feminine matrix of creation and rejuvenation—and find your personal mantra.

Because Luna is invisible while in her dark phase, we'll take our cue from her and seek out the shadows. You'll be creating a comforting blanket fort that will delight the child within you.

BONUS: Find three other friends who also want to perform this ritual. After doing it separately, come together at the Full Moon two weeks later and share your experience and insights.

You Will Need:

- a dark, quiet place where you won't be disturbed
- 4 to 6 chairs of equal size
- 1 yoga mat or comfortable pad, and a pillow
- several large blankets or quilts
- some clamps or rubber bands
- your Scheherazade altar and/or 1 deep blue candle
- hypnotic music (try Returning by Jennifer Berezan)
- your journal, a pen, and a flashlight
- 1 box of tissues

1. Bring your chairs and other supplies into the room you've chosen. Lay your mat in a central place, and position the chairs on both sides of it. Drape the blankets over them so as little light as possible gets in. Use clamps or rubber bands to attach them to the chairs. Add a comfy pillow to the mat.

2. After you're done, light the blue candle on your Scheherazade altar or in any secure spot. A glass-enclosed candle is best; it will keep your intentions burning longer. Call on Scheherazade and ask for her insights. Say something like, "Oh wise and beautiful enchantress, please bless me with your healing words and mantras. In the darkness, let me see. As I will so shall it be."

3. Turn on your hypnotic music. Make sure your phone is off. Bring your flashlight and journal with you as you crawl inside your fort. Lie down and get comfortable. Place one hand on your womb, and the other on your heart. They are your true sources of wisdom and guidance.

Breathe slowly and deeply into each center. Allow any feelings or buried memories to arise; breathe through them. Welcome any tears.

4. Imagine Scheherazade smiling at you. Feel her wise, caring presence. Ask her for your healing mantra, being as receptive as possible. Go with the first word or phrase that comes to you. If nothing comes, trust that you'll receive it later. Perhaps there's a feeling experience you're meant to have right now instead. When ready, turn on your flashlight and write in your journal. Sketch any images or words you received. Be free with your impressions and interpretations. You may wish to rest in your fort a bit longer. Reverently exit when you're ready.

5. Be alert over the next few weeks for guidance. Repeat your mantra at least three times a day. You can take your fort down or leave it up, in case you want to spend more time there.

Full Moon Ritual:
Truth-Telling

The Sun is in Sagittarius at the Gemini Full Moon. These are the signs of communication and truth-telling. In this ritual you'll come together with three female friends to do just that. These friends may or may not have performed the Gemini New Moon ritual. Just make sure that each person is trustworthy and discreet.

It's best to do this ritual at night where you can see and feel Luna watching over you. If the weather is nice, do it outdoors. You'll be sitting in a circle, either in chairs or on the ground on pillows. In the center of the circle, create a small altar with a blue, glass-enclosed candle, lapis or amethyst stones, talking stick (what you'll pass around to designate who has the floor), and anything else you like. Ask each person to bring something special for the group altar, as well as food and drink to share.

You Will Need:

- 3 like-minded friends
- chairs or pillows
- 1 blue, glass-enclosed candle
- 1 lapis or amethyst stone
- 1 talking stick
- food and drink to share

1. Go outside and raise your arms to the Full Moon. Bathe in her magical energies and ask her to bless your ritual. Say, "Hail and welcome, Scheherazade!" Each woman can ask for a blessing.

2. Sit in a circle. Pick up the talking stick and explain that each of you will be sharing a deep, perhaps secret truth about yourself. This may relate to whatever is up for you now. Share first, maybe inspired by the results of your New Moon ritual.

3. Pass the talking stick to the next person. Maintain strict silence as each person shares, listening intently to them. Then do another round in which you each share how it feels to tell the truth. For your final round, each woman poses a question that may be troubling her, and receives feedback from the others.

4. When you feel complete, go out and raise your arms again to Luna. Smooth her magic moon glow up and down your bodies. Say, "Hail and farewell, Scheherazade!" Thank her for blessing your ritual. Then it's time for feasting!

When the Moon is in Gemini

During the two-and-a-half days per month that Luna flies through the airy sign of Gemini, it feels like time is moving faster than usual. Expect a greater number of phone calls, emails, and requests you must respond to. You'll be hopping busily from one errand to the next. Although you may feel a bit scattered, your brain will be firing on all cylinders and you can get a lot done in a short amount of time. Just remember to set aside downtime, as this busy Moon can easily wear you out!

This is a good time to have meetings, write reports, get caught up with friends, take trips, and read novels or magazines. You may spend extra time on social media, posting wildly. Your extra keen wits and intelligence help you make decisions and plans. Watch for brilliant ideas that may strike out of the blue—especially while driving or traveling on a plane or train.

Gemini is a social sign, and you most likely won't want to stay home (unless you're on the dark side of your Moon). Now is the time to hang out with friends, go to parties or events, and make new contacts. Avoid gossiping, though, as it's apt to backfire. Writing in your journal or reflecting on your life can be rewarding, with insights flowing thick and fast.

It's a good time to honor your Scheherazade nature by taking a belly-dance class or spinning a mesmerizing tale for your beloved. Bonding with your mate or a close pal can be quite meaningful, with the Twins at play. Lovemaking and intimate sharing will spark laughter and delight.

THINGS TO DO WHEN THE MOON IS IN GEMINI

Give a talk or performance

Have a dialogue with your twin sides

Throw a party

Buy a car or phone
(unless Mercury is retrograde!)

Hold important meetings

Spin a beguiling story for your beloved

Read a novel

Binge-watch a comedy series

Write in your journal

Help friends solve their problems

Explore a new neighborhood

Keep your fingers busy—quilting, knitting, piano-playing

Download a new app and learn how to use it

PART 6

Moon in Cancer

My grandmother was born with her Sun and Moon in the nurturing, motherly sign of Cancer. Grandma was the ultimate homemaker. She grew cheerful daisies, made Scottish noodles from scratch, and could always be counted on for a back rub. Because she didn't drive, Grandma spent lots of time at home. She did get an ulcer (Cancer rules the stomach) by fussing and fighting with my grandfather, but she stuck by him through thick and thin.

Because the Moon is Cancer's ruling planet, if you have Moon in Cancer you too are a nurturer. You embody that sign's intuitive qualities, as well as its need for emotional security. Your strong desire to be a mom must have an outlet, whether it's raising kids, planting flowers, or starting a business. You need to feel needed, perhaps by rescuing animals or having people over for nourishing meals.

Your Lunar Superpower

Your loyalty to who or what you care for is your greatest strength. Home and heritage are sacred to your Cancer Moon. Like Ashley Callingbull, the first aboriginal woman to win the Mrs. Universe pageant, you'll fight like a mama bear for your people. Ignoring critics, Ashley Callingbull used her platform to bring attention to her long-abused Cree Nation brethren.

Because Cancer is ruled by the changeable Moon, you sense your Moon Mama's fluctuating rhythms deep in your body. This makes you ultra-sensitive and empathetic toward all creation. But you may be moody—one day up, the next day down. Your heart can easily be wounded, and you need plenty of time in your cozy nest to recuperate. Dropping deep into your inner well through warm baths, meditation, knitting, basking in the moonlight, or walking near the water's edge will rejuvenate you.

Your Lunar Shadow

Your sensitive nature makes you take things personally. When people are thoughtless, it hurts you deeply and you often have a hard time forgiving them. You need to cultivate a bit of detachment and remember that what other people say and do says more about them than it does about you.

Your Moon craves security and comfort, and because you love good food and cooking, overeating can be a problem. If you're a nervous eater or have trouble turning away goodies, make sure you're nurturing yourself properly by getting enough sleep, sex, support, and downtime so you'll feel less need to overindulge.

Cancer Moons have trouble saying no to more than just food. Learning to maintain boundaries is essential for you. Just because you feel sorry for someone doesn't mean you're obligated to give them your time, money, or sympathy, especially when your intuition advises, "Just say no."

Your Sexual Nature

Lovemaking is a nurturing experience for you; it's about sharing feelings and giving and receiving love. If there's no emotional connection, you won't be interested for long. Sex needs to be passionate for you, but you enjoy spooning together or eating ice cream post-coitus almost as much. Safety and security are essential, and your partner must be sensitive to your moods and emotional needs. Cancer Moons get attached quickly, especially once you've had sex. Your unions tend to be enduring. But you often mother your partners, and need to make sure you choose one who's your equal.

You likely had a few short-lived encounters when you were younger that proved that not everyone is as loving and faithful as you are. The watery Moons (Cancer, Scorpio, Pisces) share your need for emotional depth. The earthy Moons (Taurus, Virgo, Capricorn) can provide stability and hold a safe container for your moods and feelings.

Your Karmic Path

You have the soul of a mother. In other lifetimes, you were a maternal Goddess—queen of the homestead. In fact, you were such a dedicated wife and mom that you never got to know yourself as an individual. Being out in the world may have scared you or left you feeling exposed.

In this life, you're learning to balance your need for a homey refuge with your growing desire to make an impact on the world. That might mean delaying having a family until you've established yourself in your career. Or, perhaps you'll opt out of motherhood this time around and channel your nurturing energies into your career, pets, or volunteer efforts. Either way, make this a lifetime in which you find inner security through self-knowledge—and try to not be so affected by what others say and do.

Cancer Moon Women

Your Cancer Moon helps you make friends easily. People sense you can be counted on to come through for them. Even if you don't have children, you're the mother figure that everybody turns to for help. "One big happy family" is your motto. A Cancer Moon pal of mine considers her church her family. She sings in the choir, bakes for fundraisers, and spreads cheer to all.

Because you are a people-person with a big heart, you'd make a great therapist, nurse, social worker, or teacher. You especially love to support other women. I know one Cancer Moon woman who ran a cozy, welcoming metaphysical bookshop for years, where she served tea, held classes, and nurtured community. Another created a networking hub and workspace where women flock to support each others' businesses.

Your Cancer Moon has a natural affinity with the divine feminine, and connecting with the indigenous world can be fulfilling for you. Linda Savage, a shamanic practitioner, says she first got in touch with the Great Mother by breast-feeding her daughters. During the healing weekends she leads, Linda now

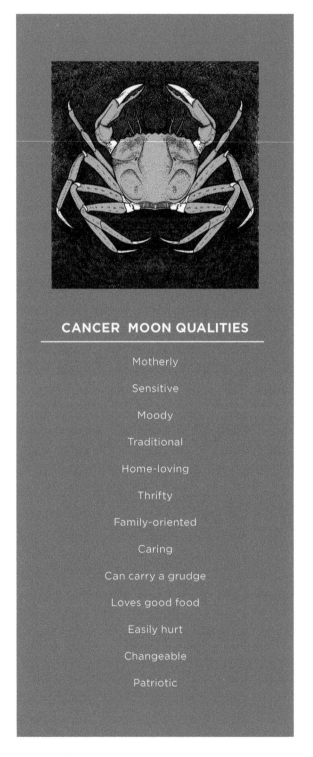

CANCER MOON QUALITIES

Motherly

Sensitive

Moody

Traditional

Home-loving

Thrifty

Family-oriented

Caring

Can carry a grudge

Loves good food

Easily hurt

Changeable

Patriotic

uses her Cancer Moon to create a safe, womb-like space for women to share with one another around a South American mesa, or altar. Yoga, ecstatic dancing, and shamanic journeying help participants bond deeply with their inner Goddess and each other.

Isis's Sacred Animal: The Dolphin

There are many creatures associated with Isis, including the scarab beetle, cat, dog, cow, and hawk. And, the traditional symbol for sensitive water sign Cancer is the crab, with its protective shell. If you resonate strongly with any of those, add representations of them to your altar. I see the dolphin as Isis's totem because the word *dolphin* comes from delphinos, or womb—the ultimate Cancer symbol. As Mama Moon Goddess Isis lights up the waves of the sea, the playful dolphin dances with her, doing back flips and deep dives into the oceanic womb of life.

If you've ever had a close-up encounter with a dolphin, you know that these mammals have an otherworldly intelligence. Along with chimps and elephants, they possess a brain that's comparable to ours. Dolphins communicate with each other in a complex language. They're friendly and protective to humans, often rescuing swimmers from sharks and other dangers.

Dolphins travel in tight, Cancerian family units known as pods. They mate for life, although females often return to their mothers' pods when they need help raising their young. These mama pods also include elderly dolphins that need protection.

The magical dolphin embodies the healing power of love, play, and laughter. Let it inspire you to relax and enjoy life while floating in Mama Isis's protective womb-space. Allow deep pleasure to undulate through your body in soft, rippling waves—and bring you home to yourself.

It would be particularly inspiring to take a dolphin trip during a Cancer Moon (preferably on the open sea rather than to a marine park). If that's not possible, you can call upon your spirit dolphin to help you with the part of your chart where Cancer is located—or whatever is troubling you. You might wish to play a recording of dolphin sounds while soaking in an Epsom salt bath (to approximate the ocean). Imagine yourself inside the sleek body of this agile creature, leaping and cavorting, as all concerns fade away. And listen for any guidance you may receive.

Ancient Cancer Moon Goddess: Isis

Isis is a living Goddess. I experienced her power some years ago at the Temple of Dendur, a small, sandstone Egyptian shrine that once stood near the Nile River and now occupies a wing of the Metropolitan Museum of Art. As I approached the shrine, I felt a huge wave of energy undulating from it. It was so intense that I began to sob. My body somehow remembered the ancient worship.

Though Isis played many roles, her status as Divine Mother is best known. She is our Ancient Cancer Moon Goddess because the motherly sign of Cancer is Moon-ruled— and so is Isis, the Mother of All. She's also called the Great Sorceress because she grew magical wings to bring her husband Osiris back from the dead and conceive their divine child, Horus. Isis's labor was difficult but fruitful; women in childbirth have long prayed for her aid.

So great was Isis's power that she was also known in Egypt and throughout the ancient world as a Goddess of love, healing, the Moon, and the sea. Her worship is the most widespread of any other female deity, and is still practiced by many devotees.

If you have Moon in Cancer, you are a daughter of Isis and may feel a special connection to her. You'll find inspiration for worshiping this potent Moon Goddess in the novels of Dion Fortune, especially Moon Magic and The Sea Priestess (two of my favorite books). A direct transmission from Isis to the author, this wisdom can't be found any-where else.

You can invoke Isis when the Moon is in Cancer or at the Summer Solstice, a powerful turning point when the Sun enters that motherly sign. If you know where Cancer falls in your natal chart, you can call on Isis's help in that area of life. Or, just ask for guidance on anything that concerns you. If you're lucky enough to have an ocean or river nearby, sit by the shore and ask Mother Isis for help (water rules the emotions). Isis can soothe and comfort you, or guide you to your next step. If you're concerned about a relationship, call on her mate, Osiris, as well. Ask the divine couple to bless and heal your union in whatever way they see fit.

Creating an Altar to Isis

Your altar to Mother Goddess Isis should contain elements that mirror Luna's radiance. Find a pale, diaphanous piece of fabric to drape across or above your altar. Add lunar symbols, such as a crescent Moon, moonstones, or a framed picture of Luna. Since the Moon and the sea are mystically connected, you could add a bowl of seawater or a dolphin image. Here are some additional possibilities; use your imagination!

You'll be using this altar in the Moon rituals that follow, but you can create it now (ideally when the Moon is in Cancer) and consecrate it to Isis. Bathrooms and kitchens are ideal for Isis altars, because they are the places in your home where water flows. But anyplace that feels right will do. Begin by draping your luminescent fabric atop a table or other surface, then add the other elements in any way that pleases you. Light some cedar or pine incense (or use a diffuser with cedar or pine oil). Place the milk or bread on the altar. Then dip your fingers into the saltwater and flick them over your heart and womb space. Call Isis's name and bid her welcome. Ask for her help with anything you may need, then watch for inner promptings or "coincidences" over the next few days.

You Will Need:

- silver stars, jewelry, or coins
- moonstones, quartz crystals, or pearls
- scented bath salts (Isis loved her baths)
- small bowl of seawater or salted water
- statue of Isis
- moon symbols of any kind
- dolphin statue or image
- Egyptian ankh or scarab beetle
- cedar or pine incense
- offerings of white foods, such as milk and bread
- white or silver candles
- a plaque or an image of Isis and Osiris

New Moon Ritual:
Your Inner Child

Because Cancer is associated with the past, it's time to revisit the child you once were—and still are, deep inside. Your inner child is very much alive and influences your life in myriad ways. She's the source of your playfulness and innocence, as well as your ability to be in the moment. But she's also very sensitive, and she overreacts at times. If she feels threatened, a mood can swamp you for the rest of the day, or even send you to bed. Someone's thoughtless remark triggers a bad memory, and suddenly you're a mess. Especially if your Moon is in Cancer, you may try to hide the feeling—but it will come out somehow, often via symptoms such as stomachaches, migraines, or female troubles.

At the Cancer New Moon, it's time to get reacquainted with your inner child and give her some much-needed love. First, find a doll that reminds you of yourself when you were young. Perhaps she has the same color hair or wears a dress that's similar to one you once had. Your surrogate self should be cuddly and big enough to hug (a Barbie doll is too small). If you have childhood jewelry or mementos, you can adorn her with them if you like. If you've already made an Isis altar, place your doll on it to receive the Mother Goddess's blessing before your ritual.

The first step of this ritual is to identify your deepest pain, which most likely originated in your childhood. Perhaps you're thinking, why should I wallow in that pain? Why not just forget it and move on? Because it's still alive in you, wreaking havoc in ways you might not suspect (e.g., health problems or relationship issues).

But as they say, if you can feel it, you can heal it. It might be as simple as something unkind a classmate once said that still returns to haunt you, or as complicated as parental abuse. If it's the latter, you may need a therapist's help. But you can still befriend your inner child and become her ally.

You Will Need:

- a quiet place where you won't be disturbed
- 1 white candle, on your Isis altar if you've made one
- 1 doll that reminds you of yourself
- 1 comfy chair
- your journal and a pen
- 1 box of tissues

1. If you've made an Isis altar, light a candle on it and ask for her help. Just call her name and ask for her blessing. Thank her for comforting and healing you.

2. Then take your journal and doll, and sit in the comfy chair. Ask her what she needs from you. See if you can sense her answer. She might be angry or sad. If so, give voice to that. Grieve or rage if necessary. A memory may flash before your eyes; tell your inner child you're so sorry for what happened to her, that you feel her pain and will comfort and protect her from here on out.

3. You may want to journal about your exchange as you go along, or wait until you're complete. Either way, let her know you're listening. Call her by your childhood nickname. Hold her close. You may be surprised how many emotions come up. If you don't feel anything, you may need to gain her trust over time. Get clear on your inner child's needs. Perhaps she wants to spend more time playing or visiting with friends. Maybe she just wants more time with you. Promise her you will follow through, and do so. When you're done, write in your journal about the experience.

4. Then give your doll a big hug and find a spot for her in plain sight—maybe a bed or dresser, or on your altar. This will remind you that she is present and needs you. Blow out the candle and thank Isis for her help.

It may take time to build a relationship with your inner child, especially if you've neglected her. You may have to sit in that cozy chair with her every day for a while until she starts to respond. But you'll know when she does, as you'll start to feel lighter, more clear, relaxed, and open. Family relations or health problems may improve. Perhaps you won't crave problematic foods so much.

A final idea: Your inner child might need a companion. Why not find her an adorable stuffed animal, as I did for my doll? Now she looks so happy with her monkey pal, who's just her size. Bonus points for finding a stuffed dolphin to keep your doll company!

Full Moon Ritual:
A Nurturing Feast

In our attempt to be all things to all people, women have become pretty darn good at giving. In this ritual, you'll experience what it's like to receive. Receiving is a feminine art that's fallen out of fashion. Sure, you receive when you get your nails or hair done. But receiving in a ritual context helps anchor the experience on a deeper level in your body.

You will be honoring Great Mother Isis and her divine partner Osiris. Although it would be nice to do this rite with your mate, it doesn't matter whether your ritual partner is male or female. We all have an inner man and inner woman. During this process you'll be honoring the receptive, feminine power within each other. The sacred masculine's role here is primarily to hold a safe container for the feminine.

You Will Need:

- lunar food and drink
- 1 dining table set with white plates, napkins, silver, and goblets
- a willing partner
- 2 moonstones
- 2 white taper candles in holders
- your journal and a pen

1. You can keep this simple and serve only a few lunar foods or go all out and create a feast. Either way, the food and drink you choose should be mostly white or light-colored, and as fresh and healthy as possible. Round or crescent-shaped foods are a great choice. Suggestions: Scallops, blanched almonds, coconut meat, date rolls with coconut covering, or honey-cakes. Milk is sacred to Isis (including rice, almond, or coconut milk). Prepare the food earlier in the day, so you can do your ritual at night when Luna is rising. Set a beautiful table, with your white plates and napkins, silverware, goblets, and white or silver candles.

2. Once the Moon has risen, take your moonstones and go outside with your partner; give one to him or her. Hold the stones in your dominant hands. Raise your arms to Luna. Salute her with, "Hail and welcome, Isis!" Draw her magic in with your breath, then lower your arms and blow the energy into the moonstone. You might feel it start to throb. Stand in silence and be receptive; Isis may have a message for either of you. Then go inside, place your moonstones next to the candles, and light the wicks. Reverently put your Moon food on the table.

3. Sit opposite each other. Acknowledge each other with your hands in prayer position, saying Namaste. Offer your partner a morsel of food from your fork or fingers, as you embody Moon Mama Isis. You are the nurturer of all life. Center yourself in your belly and give from that

sacred place. Your partner slowly receives the food, savoring it in silence. Then switch roles. As Great Mama Isis, your partner takes a morsel of food and feeds it to you.

4. If you feel like continuing the food-and-drink exchange for a while, do so. You can make it more playful at this point. When you feel complete, fill your plates with lunar delights and feast. After eating, share how the ritual exchange was for you. Was it easy or hard to receive the nourishment? Was there a particular moment where you or your partner felt Isis's presence? Did either of you receive a message?

5. After you've cleared the table, take a sampling of the food and go back outside together. Place the food in the moonlight as an offering, and thank Isis for participating in your ritual. Raise your arms to your Moon Mama and salute her, saying, "Hail and farewell, Isis!" Breathe in her radiance and feel her blessing.

6. Go inside and blow out the candles. Put the sacred food away. Then do whatever you feel inspired to do—perhaps put on music and dance or massage each other. Put the moonstone on your altar. You may want to turn it into a powerful piece of jewelry; your partner might like to do the same. Write in your journal about the experience before going to sleep.

When The Moon Is In Cancer

We like to nest when the Moon is in Cancer. You may have a hard time prying people (including yourself) out of their comfort zones, especially on weekends. We're just too tempted to sleep in, hang with our homies, get caught up on chores, or lose ourselves in a good book or movie.

If you've been meaning to bake goodies or make a pot of soup, now is the time. Family get-togethers are also favored. Visit Grandma and take her some cookies, or have the clan over for a meal. Nurture your Moon with food and drink that feed your soul, but hopefully don't expand your waistline too much.

If you're working on a Cancer Moon day, be aware that folks may be extra touchy. Give someone a well-deserved pat on the back, talk to a workmate about her family troubles, or include an outsider at lunch. Be sure everyone feels like part of the team.

Cancer needs a secure place to put down roots, and that means home. This could be a good time to put a down-payment on a house, redecorate, or move. Those in the real estate field may see an upsurge in new listings or sales. Give your home a little loving attention now. Burn some sage to clear the atmosphere, let go of clutter that's blocking your energy, or organize a family cleaning day.

Most of all, pay attention to your feelings. You will be more sensitive than usual and perhaps prone to tears. Nostalgic memories may arise. Let yourself grieve, and honor the memory of those you've lost. Look through old photo albums, re-read journals, visit places from the past, or contact old friends to regain the feeling of closeness and family.

THINGS TO DO WHEN THE MOON IS IN CANCER

Make nourishing food

Clean and decorate your home

Contact or visit relatives

Explore your family tree

Nurture the plants in your garden

Give your kids extra attention

Visit the seashore

Take a long, scented bath

Frame and hang family photos

Have a good cry

Visit the cemetery, honor your ancestors

Watch a family-style or romantic movie

Get in touch with old friends

Play with dolls, pets, and/or your inner child

PART 7

Moon in Leo

A few years ago for a feng shui project, I asked a Leo Moon friend to purge her closet and report back on the results. She threw herself into cleaning and reorganizing the space. Then, she stepped into her closet behind the gold fabric curtain. As if coming out on stage, she flung back the curtain and sang out her private intention. Suddenly she felt inspired to paint her outdoor shower a vivid purple—which stimulated a flood of fresh ideas on a book she was writing.

Like my friend, if you were born with Leo Moon you do things with flair and panache. You have a theatrical nature—even if it only comes out behind closed doors or at certain times of the month (such as when the Moon is in Leo). Your distinctive flair is also quite sensual, and often shows up in the unique way you dress and move your body. You draw people in with your instinct for fun and the sensuous vibe you radiate.

Your Lunar Superpower

Your greatest strength is your over-the-top creativity. Ruled by the Sun, Leo is a passionate fire sign that naturally shares its abundant warmth and self-expression. You need outlets to pour your creative energy into. A boring, pedestrian job or lifestyle is not for you, which is why we see many Leo Moons working in artistic fields. You would do well in a creative profession such as photography, interior design, or dance.

You're a child at heart and typically love children, so making frequent play-dates with your kids or someone else's would be fun for you. Or, you can do as Julia Cameron suggests in her book *The Artist's Way* and take yourself on regular "artist dates." These fun outings can be as simple as a walk in the park to admire the flowers, or as elaborate as meeting friends for high tea and going to see the latest art exhibition.

Your Lunar Shadow

Pride and ego can be your downfall. Leo loves to be right, and you can fight to the death for an opinion you hold dear. You may be resentful when others try to give you advice. You know what you want and rarely second- guess yourself, but you can still benefit from a little honest input. You believe in speaking out against what angers you, though that can sometimes backfire as your words come back to haunt you.

Your innate sense of authority can also be a double-edged sword. You naturally take charge of matters, which could make others feel bossed or slighted. Some Leo Moons try to get away with things, assuming their charming nature will prevail. As you move forward on a spiritual path, you will feel less need to get your way or to make a big impression on others. The more you connect with your radiant heart and practice self-love, the more people will see—and be captivated by—the real you. Letting your creative juices flow will also help keep your heart open.

Your Sexual Nature

Sex is like a movie in which you're the star, being adored by your beloved. You need to feel beautiful, so surround yourself with candles and flowers. You also like to be swept off your feet—and may enjoy doing the same to your partner. Basically, you need a king to your queen. You may have a streak of exhibitionism or enjoy playing games in bed. Going out dancing is a great prelude to the uninhibited sex you adore.

You need a partner who is capable of feeling as deeply as you do, and is willing to give you lots of attention and devotion. You like to plan exciting dates, such as hot air balloon rides and picnics in the park. When your partner does the same for you, you feel special, which sets you free to express your love in return. A mate who doesn't put you front and center won't last long in your life. If single, treat yourself to the kind of pleasures you'd like to receive from a partner. You'd adore other fiery Moons (Aries, Leo, Sagittarius) because they share your adventurous spirit. Fun, intelligent airy Moons (Gemini, Libra, Aquarius) could also be a good match—if they can get out of their heads and into their instincts.

Your Karmic Path

You have the soul of a queen. In past lives, you were royalty—or the equivalent thereof. You might even have royal blood in your lineage. You were no doubt adored and received special treatment, perhaps because of your unique talents. You may have disdained "commoners" or felt out of touch with the people. In this life, you're challenged to come down off your throne and mingle with the masses. You'll always be a queen, but to grow on a soul level you must relinquish any sense of entitlement and take second billing sometimes. Give others credit and praise them for their talents. Volunteering to help the needy is also good therapy for you. Giving back will help balance the karmic scales.

Leo Moon Women

There is something special about a Leo Moon woman that sets you apart from the crowd. You are inherently confident, and, easily rise to the top of the heap. Your regal nature is seen in the way you carry yourself and how quickly you assume control. Not surprisingly, both Queen Elizabeth II and former prime minister Margaret Thatcher have Moon in Leo.

Many compelling performers also have this placement, such as Julia Roberts with her mega-watt smile. Like her, you radiate sunny energy to all. You're naturally funny, generous, and good-natured, unless you've been beaten down too much by life. But even then, your spark can never be fully extinguished—it's part of your eternal Goddess nature.

You tend to be extravagant and like to surround yourself with beautiful things that befit your status as a queen. Your Leo Moon also has a gift for self-adornment. One Leo Moon friend, who cut her teeth on Grateful Dead concerts, still dresses up in colorful wigs and artsy costumes for music festivals, where she parties with her friends until the break of dawn. That's another thing about your Moon sign—even if you have a shy, private side, you are often front and center at festive events. You usually have lots of friends and are quite popular.

Whether or not you're born into wealth, you have an instinct for creating it. When you display your lavish talents and eye for beauty to the world, you're likely to be rewarded. I know one Leo Moon woman who owns a luxurious, European-style boutique. Another creates colorful, eye-catching websites for clients; yet another is a gifted acupuncturist who uses Tibetan bells and tuning forks in her practice.

Although all Leo Moons are creative, some prefer to downplay their flashy side. A Leo Moon writer friend told me that in kindergarten, she discovered she had a natural ease in front of large crowds. Yet, she confided that whenever she won a school election or an award, the attention made her want to crawl out of her skin. She wanted recognition, but squirmed when she got it.

In later years, when this woman saw others soaking up the spotlight, she considered their exhibitions shameful. It wasn't until she accepted her Leo Moon's desire for recognition that her natural confidence began to emerge and she finally started to identify as an artist. Now she happily expresses her regal nature—and admits that she's a sucker for a man who says he'll treat her like a queen!

LEO MOON QUALITIES

Sensual

Generous

Loyal

Queenly

Dramatic

Creative

Take-charge

Extravagant

Childlike

Self-focused

Determined

Outspoken

Oshun's Sacred Animal: The Peacock

A large, colorful pheasant renowned for his impressive iridescent tail, the male peacock uses his natural splendor to attract female peahens. Though most common to Southeast Asia, a lesser-known species of peafowl inhabits the Democratic Republic of the Congo, where native Congolese headdresses display long feathers from this regal creature.

The peacock is Oshun's totem not only for its extravagant beauty, but also its bravery. Oshun once took the form of a peacock and flew to heaven to discuss a problem with Olofi, the great creator. The other orishas (deities) had refused to go, as they knew the sun would burn them up. And indeed, as the peacock flew closer to the sun, its feathers were charred and its beauty destroyed. But Olofi was so impressed with Oshun's brave act that he made her his favorite.

The moral of this story? True beauty comes from within. Even if you're not the most gorgeous creature, or if your beauty has dimmed with age or infirmity, your Leo Moon can still enchant. Your appetite for life, love for beauty, and desire to be creative remain very much alive.

Preferably at the Leo Moon, invoke the peacock as your spirit animal by holding an image of a peacock or its feather in your hands and breathing in the power. Or, visit a zoo or wildlife refuge where peacocks live and admire their beauty. See if you can feel a resonance within yourself. If you have a peacock feather, place it under your pillow at night and ask your spirit animal to visit in a dream. Keep your journal by your bed so you can record the results—along with any messages you may receive.

Ancient Leo Moon Goddess: *Oshun*

Oshun is the Goddess of love in the West African Yoruba religion, which spread to Brazil and the Caribbean during slavery times. Sometimes called the "African Venus," Oshun is the queen of performing arts and personal adornment. Just like the Leo Moon woman, she radiates beauty and delight, and she knows her own power and worth.

Oshun sparkles and refreshes like the river. Wearing a yellow silk gown with tinkling bells at the hem and jewelry of gold and amber, she walks with undulating grace, and her sensual dance captivates all. None can resist her lush, womanly figure and honeyed lips.

If your Moon is in Leo, you are a daughter of Oshun. You share her generosity, gay spirit, and love for life. Your natural sweetness, warmth, and wit easily attract admirers who want to be near you. Yoruba priestess Luisah Teish, herself a daughter of Oshun, waxes poetic about her Mama in her book Jambalaya. She says that when Oshun perfumes her skin with honey no one can resist, and urges us to surrender to her passion and let it kindle a warm, sultry fire within us.

Oshun is a charmer who often succeeds where others fail by using her feminine wiles. She's not immune to misfortune, however, and it can render her melancholy at times. Like those with Moon in Leo, she can be willful, even vindictive when crossed. A spoonful of sugar (or better yet, honey!) goes a long way toward keeping her happy.

It's best to invoke Oshun when the Moon is in Leo, or when visiting a flowing body of water (her native habitat). Oshun can make you feel beautiful and powerful, so be sure to light a candle to her before going on a date or giving an important presentation. Rub a bit of honey on the candle before lighting it, and put a drop on your tongue before calling Oshun's name. Then ask that she bless whatever you're about to do.

Creating an Altar to Oshun

The purpose of this altar is to enchant the Love Goddess in you, so make it as beautiful as possible. Start with a piece of yellow silk or luminous gold fabric. Add a jar of honey, beautiful jewelry, and a pair of yellow or gold candles. The number five is sacred to Oshun, so include a bowl of nickels. Cowrie shells, shaped like a vulva, are beloved by her. Even if you can't find all these items, just be creative and have fun.

Once you've set up your altar, arranging the elements until you're satisfied with the results, consecrate it during a Leo Moon. Light the candles and incense and turn on some lively music, perhaps with drums. Call Oshun's name and do a little dance for her. You'll be performing a more elaborate ritual of this kind at the Leo New Moon, but it's good to let Oshun know ahead of time that you intend to honor her. If you have a special request, speak it out loud and give thanks for her help with it.

You Will Need:

- 1 yellow silk or metallic gold altar cloth
- 1 jar of honey, perhaps with cinnamon sticks in it
- fresh flowers, ideally yellow daisies or sunflowers
- 1 handheld mirror, for the Goddess to admire herself
- 1 bowl of nickels and/or river water
- perfume, sandalwood or vetiver incense
- 2 yellow or gold candles
- 1 image of Oshun
- beautiful jewelry, especially coral, amber, gold, and brass
- cowrie shells
- 1 beautiful fan
- pumpkin, winter squash, oranges, or lemons
- peacock feathers, if you can find them

New Moon Ritual:
Self-Enchantment

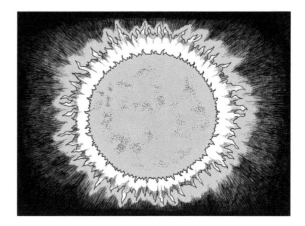

We all need more love in our lives. And because the Leo New Moon is a time for new beginnings, you'll be petitioning Oshun for a fresh start with love in this ritual. This starts with opening your heart more fully. Love is truly all around us, but often we don't see (or feel) it because of the walls we've built around our hearts from past hurts or limiting beliefs about ourselves. This can lead to feeling dispirited, as if you have lost the magnetism that lures positive people and events to you. Let Oshun help you feel beautiful, powerful, and magnetic once more.

For those of us in the Northern Hemisphere, the Leo New Moon happens in the summer, when the sun, Leo's ruler, is at its strongest. So it's a perfect time to relax and open to your sunny, sensual nature—and enjoy wearing a sexy summer dress!

You Will Need:

- lavender bath salts or bath oil
- 2 yellow or gold candles
- essential oils or your favorite perfume
- 1 yellow or gold dress that shows off your figure and optional sash
- 1 gold necklace, perhaps with coral or amber beads or stones
- 1 full-length mirror and sensual music with a beat
- your Oshun altar
- 1 glass jar of high-quality honey
- cinnamon sticks, whole cloves, and whole nutmeg
- 1 lace or feathered fan if you have one

1. In this ritual you'll be honoring your body and your deep, sensual nature. Begin by taking a ritual bath with lavender salts or oil. You may wish to burn candles around the tub, especially if you're doing this at night. As you soak, relax and let go. Imagine all cares floating away. In particular, release any stress around your relationship to your body—from aches and pains to disapproval of what you may see as your flaws. After bathing, blow out the candles and anoint yourself with essential oils or perfume. Adorn yourself with makeup if you wish. Put on your pretty dress and jewelry you love, especially if it's gold, amber, or coral. You might want to wrap a sash around your hips or head.

2. Turn on your sensual music and go to your Oshun altar. Light the candles and praise Oshun for her beauty and kindness. Ask her to inhabit your body and soul. Then open the jar of honey and "fix" it (in the old southern parlance) with the cinnamon sticks, whole cloves, and nutmeg. Dip your finger in the honey and have a taste, bringing Oshun's sweet, healing magic into your body and soul.

3. Take your fan, if you have one, and stand in front of the full-length mirror. Admire your beauty. Praise the parts of you that you love, whether they include your long neck, strong legs, or ample bosom. Send love to the parts you dislike. Take some deep breaths as you let your body sway to the music. Move your hips, undulating like a snake. Enchant yourself. Move the fan slowly, sensually around your body.

4. When you feel complete, go back to your altar and thank Oshun for her participation and blessings. Continue to honor this sensual Moon in whatever way feels right. Cook a nice dinner, make love with your mate, do an art project, write in your journal, sleep naked. Oshun is alive in you now—look for signals she may send in the next few days, and be sure to honor any impulses to create more pleasure in your life. Leave your altar up for at least two weeks, as you'll need to use it again at the Leo Full Moon. In the meantime, light a candle to Oshun each day in the morning.

Full Moon Ritual:
Invoking for Love

The Leo Full Moon happens when the Sun is in experimental Aquarius. Now's the time to try something a little bit daring. This ritual is inspired by the voodoo tradition, which has its roots in West Africa and migrated to places such as Cuba, Haiti, and New Orleans, along with the slaves.

Now you'll be invoking for love, whether in the form of a new partner or to improve your existing union. It's best not to focus on securing the love of someone who's already taken, however, as that can create bad juju. If you're seeking a new love, first write down exactly what you want to experience in the relationship, and what kind of person you want him (or her) to be. You might write something like, "He puts me at the center of his world," or "Together we live a healthy and fit lifestyle." Avoid negative statements such as "He's not an alcoholic and doesn't beat me." Take some time with this, as you don't want to attract the wrong person. Focus on how you want to feel in the relationship. To improve your current partnership, write down how you'd like it to look and feel.

You Will Need:

- 1 round mirror big enough to hold 5 small candles
- your Oshun altar
- sandalwood oil
- some high-quality honey
- your statement of intent
- 5 nickels
- red rose petals
- 5 small yellow or pink candles enclosed in glass
- 1 spade for digging
- 1 jar of spring water

1. Do this ritual on a Friday night as close to the waxing Full Moon as possible (Friday is sacred to Oshun). Set the mirror on your Oshun altar and anoint it with sandalwood oil and honey. On top of that, place the folded-up paper on which you've written what you desire. You may need to tape it together to keep it flat. Put the five nickels on top of that (five is Oshun's number), and add the rose petals. Place the candles in a circle around the mirror. As you light them, call Oshun's name.

2. Go outside and set the mirror with candles under the Full Moon. Make sure it's secure and protected from the elements. Raise your arms and draw down Luna's power until you feel her magic tingling in your veins. Then affirm, "Magical forces now conspire to send me my heart's desire!"

3. While the candles burn, do something sensual to honor Oshun, such as dance to your favorite music. Once the candles have burned down, dig a hole and bury everything but the mirror. Pour the jar of spring water over it. Then give Oshun some time to attend to your request. Leave offerings of milk, honey, or flowers on her altar until you receive the desired results. Meanwhile, clean your house and prepare yourself for love. Buy a new outfit or get a facial. Heed any intuitive promptings, such as a place to visit, party to attend, or conversation to initiate.

When The Moon Is In Leo

Like all days when the Moon is in a fire sign, Leo Moons are full of action. This period is great for tackling big projects, working out, giving a talk, shopping for beautiful items, or entertaining friends. If you have Moon in Leo, you'll feel like making things happen—and you won't be able to contain your vibrant, sparkly nature.

No matter your Moon sign, this time of the month offers an opportunity to shine. Schedule important meetings or presentations now. Also, play-dates—or even a first date—are apt to go well. You should find success visiting a new hairstylist, and you might even come home with something more colorful or daring than you'd had in mind!

Opening nights and theatrical events are tailor-made for the Moon in Leo. It's also a great time for anything involving children—from a soccer game to a birthday party or a benefit walk for kids. Your childlike nature will come out too, so make sure you have some fun activities scheduled to offset any work obligations.

Some folks may tend to act out now, however. You might see more displays of pique or willfulness, especially from those in authority. If you have Moon in Leo, find a creative or physical outlet in which to channel your fire. Otherwise, you run the risk of bossing others or taking charge of things in a way that could be alienating. This is a great Moon under which to paint or write, redecorate the house, organize your office, or go out dancing—you should have energy to burn.

There's a sexy, romantic vibe at the Leo Moon, so schedule some quality time with your partner or go out someplace fun and do a little flirting. Lovemaking can be great under Leo Moon—as long as there's genuine affection involved and each person is made to feel special.

THINGS TO DO WHEN THE MOON IS IN LEO

Make love

Give a talk or presentation

Get dressed up and go out dancing

Take a vacation

Have a heart-to-heart talk
with a loved one

Buy new clothes or jewelry

Go to an art opening

Run or work out

Paint, draw, or color

Host a party or go to one

Pitch a creative idea

Watch your temper

Tackle a big project

Toot your own horn

Get a spa treatment

PART 8

Moon in Virgo

Early on, I studied with an astrologer who would invite a special guest to each class. This person allowed us to dissect their natal chart and ask probing questions. The guest I remember most vividly was a successful porn star. An unassuming woman with Moon (and several other planets) in Virgo, she'd spend a few days a month making an explicit film, then retreat to her rustic canyon home, where she lived like a hermit with her dogs. She'd realized long ago that she wasn't cut out for marriage. She was just too independent—but she loved sex. So she found work that fed her sensuality, paid the bills, and gave her plenty of time to herself.

If you have Moon in Virgo, you may not choose to live this woman's lifestyle, but I'll bet you found her story intriguing. You're just as self-reliant and sensual as she is, though you may express it differently.

Your Lunar Superpower

Your earthy sensuality is your greatest strength. Sex is likely important to you, but with a sacred bent. You sense that you're healing yourself and your partner through that primal connection.

In relationships, you need someone who respects your independent nature and gives you space, but is there to nurture you at the end of the day. You work hard to take care of your family and expect your mate to be as diligent as you are. If you stay mired in the day-to-day grind for too long, though, you'll pick each other apart. Set aside regular time for lovemaking and fun getaways to keep the romance alive.

Your Virgo Moon gives you a keen mind, precise eye for detail, and willingness to tackle complex tasks that require painstaking attention. These abilities translate well into creative fields such as photography, graphic art, or costume design—or detail-oriented occupations such as accounting.

Many Virgo Moons prefer an organic lifestyle. Virgo rules the harvest, with its picking and sorting of crops and medicinal herbs. That's where your love for health comes in. Planting a vegetable garden or growing some mint and basil in a window-box planter might appeal
to you.

Even if you indulge in junk food, your passion for health will surface at some point. Sometimes it takes a medical emergency to trigger your instinct to take care of yourself. I've seen several Virgo Moon women undertake incredibly disciplined (almost military!) health regimens and effectively heal themselves of dire conditions.

You might even make a living from your love for the natural life. A Virgo Moon friend and her husband run an organic farm that employs vets who've been traumatized in battle. As the vets work the land, their psyches begin to heal. My friend, who eradicated her own breast cancer through natural means, has effectively combined her love for healthy food, healing, and productive partnership.

Your Lunar Shadow

Fault-finding can be your downfall. You may have discovered that your keen ability to see flaws and fix them, while valuable in your work, is not much appreciated in personal relationships. Why would people take offense when you're just trying to be helpful, pointing out imperfections or correcting inaccuracies? Probably because their feelings were hurt.

You expect perfection of yourself as well and can be your own worst critic. It's good to make a habit of forgiving yourself and others when expectations aren't met, even in minor ways. Practicing yoga or ch'i gong will help get you out of your head and into your body, and make you more relaxed. Sometimes taking off your glasses is all that's needed to shift into a softer mode. Virgo is ruled by communicative Mercury; being vulnerable enough to share your feelings can work wonders.

your sexual nature

Your deepest desire is to serve your lover, and you like to plan rituals or special experiences during which you can adore each other. Beware of over-thinking things, though, as spontaneity is also necessary for a sexy experience. So what if the house isn't pin perfect when your man arrives or you're having a bad hair day? Just put on a pot of yummy soup for afterward that permeates the atmosphere with love and nourishment.

Your priestess instinct knows what to do in bed—just let the Goddess come through, and you'll amaze and delight him. You'd vibe well with the earthy Moon signs (Taurus, Virgo, Capricorn), who want to serve and worship you—and know how to take their time. The watery Moon signs (Cancer, Scorpio, Pisces) will get your passions going, satisfy your emotional needs, and often make good long-term mates.

Your Karmic Path

You have the soul of a priestess. In previous lives you were devoted to your spiritual path or work and made everything else subservient to it. You might even have taken vows of poverty or chastity, or been unable to marry. Though this path was likely heartfelt, you learned to deny yourself fulfillment through emotional involvements. This self-denial still makes it hard to connect deeply with others. Now you need to relax into the arms of the Goddess and let yourself be served. You don't have to do everything yourself anymore. Ask yourself whether your strong independent streak or need to be of service may be keeping you from letting people in or receiving help. If so, discussing this with your significant other or a potential partner can lead to greater intimacy.

Virgo Moon Women

Women with Virgo Moon (much like Virgo Sun and Ascendant) love systems and methodical activities. This makes you a great editor, scientist, doctor or teacher. You like working at home or with homes, and doing rituals in that environment. A realtor pal with a Virgo Moon does something unique at the close of each escrow. She walks through the vacant house and sings. She says it's like smudging with sage to clear the energy, but using sound vibration. She thanks the previous occupants and bids them farewell, clearing the space to receive its new residents.

Although you're not necessarily a neat freak, you do want some control over your environment. If you work at home, you may be oblivious to your surroundings while you're in work mode. But then you'll likely start to feel blocked or frustrated, and look up to discover that yet again, your house is a mess. It's time to put everything else aside and start cleaning, sorting, and releasing unneeded stuff. Then you can sit back down to work with a fresh eye and a renewed burst of inspiration.

Your Virgo Moon needs to feel connected to something greater than yourself, or you may tend to feel anxious and try too hard to control outcomes. Forging a strong, earthy relationship to the Goddess and giving things over to her will keep you grounded and secure.

Sacred sexuality teacher Lisa Schrader of Awakening Shakti describes her relationship to the Divine Mother like this: "For me, she's not far away on a cloud, remote and ethereal. She's right here, wrapping her arms around me, behind my eyes watching the candle flicker, inhaling the delicious smell of the soup simmering on the stove. She's

VIRGO MOON QUALITIES

Witty

Smart

Industrious

Opinionated

Health-oriented

Precise

Methodical

Conscientious

Service-oriented

Independent

Connected to the Earth

Devoted

intimate in my life, pulsing in my body, breathing on my neck."

Schrader embodies the priestess aspect of her Virgo Moon. Following her example by allowing the Goddess to embrace you in your daily life can transform tedium into transcendence.

You're a tender, devoted caretaker for those in need. You'll wait on loved ones hand and foot when they're recovering from an illness. And, you're willing to make long drives or flights to visit those you care about, even when it's inconvenient.

Because you're so often in service to others, you need regular dives into your opposite polarity. Virgo's opposite sign is watery, dreamy Pisces, which is about letting go and opening to magic. Dipping into the Pisces pool may be as simple as taking a nap at the end of a hard day, or asking someone else to do the chores. Swimming, lovemaking, and Moon-gazing are also beautiful Piscean expressions. Give your inner Goddess a timeout, then you'll be refreshed and able to return to the world.

Vesta's Sacred Animal: The Cat

Greek mythology says the donkey is Hestia's (Vesta's) sacred animal, because the braying of that creature once saved the Goddess from violation after a drunken Olympian feast. Although I love donkeys—and please put one on your altar if you want to—I don't feel this is the appropriate creature for Vesta. So I've appointed another animal as her totem: the cat.

Independent, intelligent, sensitive, and possessed of claws should she need them—just like a Virgo

Moon woman—the cat was a favorite at Goddess temples in ancient times. If you've got Moon in Virgo or are drawn to the special charms of the cat, put a feline figure on your altar.

But stay attuned to your intuition. If an owl, a wolf, a deer, or another creature visits you in a dream the night before the ritual or seems more appropriate to you, then by all means honor that creature instead. You're the priestess—claim your power and work with whatever comes to you!

You can call on your spirit cat when the Moon is in Virgo to help you gain clarity, get more organized, or clean up your act in some way (cats are notoriously clean creatures!). If you have a cat, make her a special meal, or spend extra time grooming and playing with her. Or give a donation to your local animal shelter to honor Vesta. If you know which part of your natal chart contains the sign of Virgo, ask the Goddess to bestow a special blessing for you on that area of life.

When The Moon Is In Virgo

If you're an earthy priestess with Moon in Virgo, you're more attuned than most to the vibrations of the planet. So during the two-and-a-half days each month that the Moon travels through Virgo, take time to commune with Mama Earth. This will help you stay in tune with your body and flow with any energy shifts. Putting your bare feet on the Earth or sitting on the grass will help you stay grounded and centered.

No matter your Moon sign, take extra good care of yourself during the Virgo Moon phase with healthy food, love, and healing treatments. If anxiety starts to get the best of you, that's your cue to take a timeout.

Staying mentally sharp is paramount now, so it's a good time to make green drinks or nourishing new recipes. Virgo loves shopping (it's the hunter-gatherer in you), so hit the grocery store with ingredient list in hand, and dedicate time to making healthy fare like a big pot of chili or soup, and freeze some for later.

Your mind and senses will be keener than usual when the Moon travels through precise, detail-oriented Virgo. This should help with work projects. You'll be able to see and communicate the fine points clearly, so it's a great time to write or edit a paper, have important meetings, thoroughly clean the house, do strength training, or anything that requires intensive focus.

You may be called upon to serve those in need, perhaps by bringing chicken soup to an infirm relative, covering for a sick coworker, or helping a friend move. If you start to feel frustrated with others (or they with you), avoid nitpicking and be sure to speak in positive terms.

Ancient Virgo Moon Goddess: *Vesta*

Vesta, Roman Goddess of the hearth, is one of the most powerful feminine deities. Later called Hestia by the Greeks, she's the oldest and most venerable Roman Goddess.

Roman mythology depicts Vesta as a self-contained Goddess who got a bad start in life. Imprisoned with her siblings in the bowels of hell by her jealous father, she cared for her family until they were finally liberated. Vesta swore an oath to remain eternally virgin (owned by no man), which is not surprising given her monstrous father!

Vesta sustained the people with her sacred fire, bringing warmth, nourishment, and inspiration. Her priestesses, the Vestal Virgins, were in charge of keeping alight the perpetual fire that was the mystical heart of Rome. At one point, the Vestals were known as "sacred harlots." They united with strangers and male worshipers of the Goddess, often taking in men who'd been damaged by war and restoring them to wholeness. Their sexuality was dedicated to a higher purpose. A Vestal was considered virgin, self-contained, one-in-herself.

By the fourth century C.E., threatened by their power as emancipated women, the Church snuffed out the last of the Vestals along with the six-hundred-year-old perpetual flame on Vesta's hearth. Their reputation of purity passed to the Christian nuns, also virgins consecrated to marriage with the Divine.

If you have a Virgo Moon, you're blessed by Vesta's power. The Goddess made you self-directed and independent, even if, like all of us, you sometimes find it hard to trust yourself or make your way
in life.

You can invoke Vesta's power when the Moon is in Virgo, at the Virgo New and Full Moons—or whenever you need a dose of healing and grounding. Since Vesta and Virgo are connected to agriculture, why not buy some fresh herbs and use them to brew a restorative cup of tea or make a tasty stir-fry? Drink a toast or raise a fork to Vesta. You might also light a candle to her and affirm that her eternal, healing flame burns brightly within you.

Creating an Altar to Vesta

Vesta's altar should be simple and heartfelt. This Mother Goddess is of the Earth, though her inner flame burns brightly. Therefore, your altar to her should include both Earth and fire elements.

Gather Vesta's sacred elements and arrange them in a pleasing fashion on your altar. You can set it up inside your house, or perhaps outside on your patio or in a protected area of your yard (being an earthy Goddess, Vesta loves to be close to nature). Consecrate the altar by lighting the candles and incense, and breathing in the warmth and fragrant smoke. Scatter the seeds around the altar to "seed" it with your intentions. Ask Vesta and her totem animal for whatever help or blessings you need.

You Will Need:

- 1 small bowl of earth or a healthy potted plant
- gold, red, or green candles
- sage or incense (Nag Champa is my favorite)
- 1 statue or picture (preferably framed) of Vesta
- 1 small bowl of seeds
- bougainvillea or other blossoms in a vase
- 1 image or statue of a cat

New Moon Ritual:
Fire-Gazing

If you need a dose of Virgo Moon power, try one of the following rituals. They can be done whenever you need healing and revitalization, or if you're about to begin a new work or health-related project. This first ritual is geared toward the Virgo New Moon, a time of sorting and reaping, which for most of us falls in autumn.

A contemplative Goddess, Vesta can help you enter a calm, creative right brain state. She'll help you shift into a trance-like mode—sometimes called the Zone—fairly quickly. Scrying is an ancient method of divining answers to important questions, or simply becoming centered and focused. To scry, you gaze meditatively into either water or fire and see what impressions or images come to you. As this is a ritual to Vesta, Goddess of the Hearth, we'll be using fire. You can stare into a fireplace or an outdoor fire pit, but the easiest way to do this is with a candle.

You Will Need:

- a quiet, private place
- meditative music
- your journal and a pen
- 1 piece of bread or small bowl of seeds
- 1 pillar candle (green, red, or gold), matches
- lavender or lemongrass oil
- your Vesta altar with a picture of Vesta on it
- 1 nearby sleeping cat, if possible

1. Dim the lights. Turn on the music and turn off your phone. Sit in front of your Vesta altar, with your journal and pen at hand.

2. Offer Vesta the piece of bread or bowl of seeds as an offering, and set it next to her image. Anoint the unlit candle with lavender or lemongrass oil, inhaling the fragrance. Take your time; you're entering the magical realm of the senses. Light the wick.

3. Stare into the flame and breathe deeply. Quiet your mind and relax. Allow yourself to merge with the flame. Feel its warmth flowing through your body and renewing your vitality. Regard your image of Vesta until you feel her compassionate love start to warm your heart. Thank her for being present. If you have a burning question, pose it to her. You may want to ask that she quell any anxiety and give you peace, reveal what your next course of action might be, or whether you're on the right track.

4. Soon you should start to receive impressions. They may come in the form of images in the flame or just as feelings or impulses. If nothing comes, don't worry. You may receive an answer in your dreams that night, or in an article you read in the next few days. When you feel complete, give thanks to Vesta, blow out the candle, and journal about your experience. You may want to take a nice hot bath infused with lavender oil, which will help you absorb Vesta's message more deeply.

Full Moon Ritual:
Taking Priestess Vows

The Virgo Full Moon opposes the Sun in mystical Pisces. This magical axis combines grounding earth and nourishing water, much like Virgo's symbol of wheat becomes bread, which nourishes our bodies. It's best to honor Luna in a natural setting. This could be a friend's backyard, local park, or wherever you choose. I've done many powerful rituals in a nearby park that used to be a cemetery. Just make sure you keep safety in mind because you will be going out after dark.

Virgo is the priestess Moon, so an initiation is in order. You'll be telling Vesta (or Luna, if you prefer to be more generic) that you're serious about being her priestess. Before you begin, think carefully about what this means for you. You may want to commit to taking better care of yourself or finding more fulfilling work. Or it might be time to dedicate yourself to a new spiritual path. Only commit to what you're certain you will follow through on.

You can do this ritual on your own, but it's also lovely to share it with like-minded sisters and bear witness to each other. It can be done more than once, to renew your vows.

1. You may want to print out the vow listed below, unless you prefer to memorize it or say it in your own words.

2. Put on your Goddess garb and find a spot outside where you have as clear a view of Luna as possible. Stand on the Earth (in a circle if you're in a group) and take some deep breaths to center yourself. When you feel ready, raise your hands while holding your crystal, and salute your Moon Mama. Say, "Hail and welcome, Vesta!"

You Will Need:

- Goddess garb (perhaps a long dress or cape)
- a private spot to commune with the Moon at night
- like-minded sisters, if you choose
- 1 pointed quartz crystal, at least 3 inches (8 cm) long, for each person
- food to share for feasting afterward

3. Begin to draw the lunar power down through your hands, until it fills your entire body. You may feel it as a sense of tingling or warmth in your cells. The crystal will amplify this process. Do this until you feel the power, for five minutes or so. Then set the crystal down and with your hands, smooth the Moon glow all over your body. Feel your connection to an ancient lineage of priestesses who've been worshiping Luna since the dawn of time. Once you're filled with Moon power, kneel down on the Earth and pick up your crystal. If you're in a group, do the next process one at a time, while witnessing each other.

4. Regard your crystal and say out loud (use your own words if you prefer): "Upon this glorious Full Moon night, I fully claim my power and might. With this sacred crystal by my side, I pledge my heart as Vesta's bride." (Substitute the word Luna if you choose.) Place the crystal against your heart and deeply inhale its magical energy. Raise it once more to Luna for a moment, then lower your hands. The next woman does the same. When you're complete, bid the Moon goodbye. Say, "Hail and farewell, Vesta!" then adjourn for feasting. Place your crystal on your altar. You might even want to turn it into a piece of sacred jewelry that will remind you of your commitment.

5. Over the next few days, you might get a strong urge to purge the house, organize your files, call someone, or go somewhere. You are now in Vesta's (Luna's) service; pay close attention to what she desires from you—such as how she may want to bless someone else through you.

THINGS TO DO WHEN THE MOON IS IN VIRGO

Embark on a health regimen

Begin a fitness boot camp or work-related training

Get caught up on sleep

Tidy your workspace

Volunteer with a local charity

Weed and prune your garden

Do a spring-cleaning

Make a green drink or other healthy fare

Groom the dog or cat

Send emails and create posts

Schedule counseling sessions

Nurture yourself with an Epsom salt bath

Buy vitamins or plant herbs

Schedule surgeries (unless the Moon is void)

PART 9

Moon in Libra

Libra is the lover's sign. If your Moon is in Libra, your soul is geared toward love, art, beauty, and fairness. You have an urge to unite opposites, look for similarities, and establish equilibrium. Thinking of others comes naturally to you. I know many Libra Moon women who've been happily married for a long time. In quite a few cases, these couples' kisses remain as passionate as they were at the beginning.

But not all Libra Moons are happily mated. Unmarried and a recluse for much of her life, poet Emily Dickinson maintained most of her deep connections through letter-writing. Because she ordered her letters burned after her death, we'll never know her feelings for those with whom she corresponded. Yet the lyrical poems she left behind are a testament to her Libra Moon's romantic nature. A passionate life of the mind was apparently enough to satisfy her need for love and companionship.

Your Lunar Superpower

Your greatest strength is your ability to bridge the gap with others. This stems from your desire for everyone to get a fair shake—and to be heard. Libra is the sign of the diplomat; you have an uncanny ability to bring opposing factions together. Many who campaign for social justice have Libra Moon. You instinctively stand up for what you believe is right. You'll bend over backward to help those in need, and you're very loyal. You're often the first to offer help when a friend has fallen on hard times, even to start an online campaign to raise funds. A Libra Moon woman I know took her housekeeper's daughter under her wing and has managed to accumulate enough donations to put the girl through college.

Your Lunar Shadow

Indecision is your Achilles heel; you're always weighing pros and cons and sometimes fail to take necessary action. Also, if you feel someone has done you (or someone you care for) wrong, you won't forget it anytime soon. You might hang on to unworkable relationships while waiting for the other person to change, or to pay back what they owe you. Resentment can bind you to people like glue. So can misguided hope. Have you ever fallen for the wrong guy, yet couldn't let go? Perhaps you felt sorry for him, or you'd made a promise you were loath to break. In cases like that, your strong sense of loyalty can work against you.

Your Sexual Nature

You have a deep need for love and relationships. Casual flings don't interest you; you're looking for a mate and won't settle for less than a mutually satisfying partnership. You love sex and are deeply romantic, and making love has to be a primal joining of minds and bodies. Sexy lingerie and scented candles help set the mood, as beauty is essential to you. But if your partner doesn't treat you fairly, your passion can wane. Open communication is the ultimate aphrodisiac. The air sign Moons (Gemini, Libra, Aquarius) can keep up with your agile mind and could make a great mate for you. You'd find the fire sign Moons (Aries, Leo, Sagittarius) stimulating and fun, and they can handle your occasional fierceness, but they could end up being too independent for you.

Your Karmic Path

You have the soul of a peacemaker. In other lifetimes, people turned to you to champion their cause or bring people together. You catered to others' needs and kept a smile on your face while resentment grew. You secretly longed for greater independence—more time to yourself, the ability to call the shots—but when push came to shove, you always gave in. In this lifetime, your soul is determined to find greater balance between your needs and others'. Maybe that means putting your foot down the next time your restless mate decides he wants to move, or it could mean setting better boundaries at your job. Worrying about what others may think is so past-life for you. It's time to let your inner Goddess rule!

LIBRA MOON QUALITIES

Fairness-minded

Relationship-oriented

Diplomatic

Giving

Communicative

Companionable

Artistic

Social

Witty

Self-sacrificing

Loyal

Resentful

Libra Moon Women

A Libra Moon woman has a twinkle in her eye that can snag even the most elusive man. The symbol for Libra is the balancing scales, which bring equal opposites together. Your soul yearns to be mated with the Other—usually a beloved person. But if there's no emotional give-and-take, you'll feel off-kilter. One Libra Moon woman I know stayed in a marriage that had long since died, for her daughter's sake. Once the girl graduated, so did Mom—to a new life in another state. Yet re-balancing the scales post-divorce hasn't been easy. My friend is now learning to reconnect with the most important Other in her life—herself.

Being alone doesn't come naturally for someone with Moon in Libra, yet a dose of solitude from time to time can be good medicine for you. Taking a sabbatical from relationships for a while can put you back in touch with who you are. Some Libra Moon women rely too much on their mates, wanting to be together all the time. If this is you, try stepping out on your own a bit more. You may find you like it. Libra women are deeply feminine, but also possess so-called masculine traits, such as a strong intellect, fiercely protective nature, and sense of justice.

Balance and harmony are also big themes for you. You take the covenant of marriage seriously and need to make sure you're in an equal partnership before committing. This is especially true if you've been married before and don't want your heart to be broken again. Make sure you'll be honored as the Goddess that you are.

Why not follow my friend Laura's lead, and make your prospective mate jump through a few hoops before getting serious with him? After two months of dating a new man, this Libra Moon woman had a feeling he was the one, but she wanted to be sure. So she gave him five gift cards for experiences that took him way out of his comfort zone—including energy exchange, Moon rites, and Tantric massage. Since he'd loved Laura from the moment they met, this man rose to the challenge. And they've been happily married for more than twenty years.

Creating balance extends to other areas of your life as well. Fairness is very important to you; Libra Moons can get swept up in a cause that's bigger than themselves. Many of you are doing great things in the world, righting wrongs and spearheading change. As it did for the modern Moon Goddess profiled next, your instinctive desire to fight for equality can even catapult you into a life-or-death struggle for what you believe in.

Inanna's Sacred Animal: The Lioness

In ancient art, Inanna was often depicted standing on the backs of two lionesses, who symbolize strength, fertility, and social bonding. As a Libra Moon woman, the lioness is your power animal.

Though her roar may not be as thunderous as her mate's, the lioness is just as fierce. She'll fight to the death to protect her cubs, and she often wins.

Social etiquette is very important to the lioness, just as it is to the Libra Moon woman. When lionesses of the same pride meet, they engage in a greeting ritual that involves low purring and rubbing to reaffirm their connection. If a female is disinclined to meet and greet, she's apt to be booted out of the pride.

Like most Libra Moon women, the lioness can be a flirt. When in estrus, she'll walk sensually past a male, swishing her tail, then "assume the position." The act itself is quite fierce on both sides—with him biting the nape of her neck, and her snarling and baring her teeth at him. When she's got her eye on a mate, don't mess with a lioness—or a Libra Moon woman!

You can call on the power of the lioness to save your marriage, invoke protection for your children, or mend a problematic friendship. Just meditate on the image of a lioness or watch YouTube videos to fix her energy firmly in your mind. Then ask your lioness totem for what you need and give thanks that she'll help bring about the best solution.

Ancient Libra Moon Goddess: *Inanna*

Inanna is an ancient Sumerian love and fertility Goddess. Like her Babylonian counterpart Ishtar, Inanna was said to be the life blood of the Earth. The most prominent female deity in Mesopotamia as far back as 4000 B.C.E., many temples along the Tigris and Euphrates rivers were dedicated to Inanna.

At one, known as the House of Heaven, priestesses of the Goddess united in sacred sexual communion with worshipers. Each year at the Spring Equinox, the high priestess as Inanna would ritually mate with a young man representing the shepherd Dumuzi, Inanna's consort. Sumerian kings were often crowned in this way.

Inanna was associated with the planet Venus (ruler of Libra) and its gifts of love and connectedness. Yet like Venus in its dual forms of "morning star" and "evening star," Inanna had two sides—she possessed both feminine and masculine traits. As the Goddess of love and war, she had to balance the opposing scales of her own nature. Like the Libra Moon woman, Inanna possesses an "iron fist in a velvet glove." She's capable of using her charm to get her way.

In one version of Inanna's myth, she visited the Underworld to attend a funeral—which turned out to be her own. She dressed elaborately in a gown, wig, and turban, wearing a lapis lazuli necklace and other fine jewels. As Inanna descended, she was forced to surrender each item until she was naked and stripped of power. Then her dark twin sister, Ereshkigal, turned her into a corpse and hung her on a hook to rot.

After three days, Inanna was rescued and revived. Yet being shorn of her beauty and left for dead had only amplified her powers. She'd been forced to dig deep and find the will to survive. As many Libra Moon women can attest, enduring a dark experience can make you strong.

You can invoke Inanna when the Moon is in Libra, at the Fall Equinox when the Sun enters Libra, during the Libra New or Full Moon, or whenever you need strength or a fresh start. Call Inanna's name. Eat some pomegranate seeds in her honor, and affirm that you'll make it through this trying time.

Creating an Altar to Inanna

Despite her connection to love planet Venus, hearts and flowers are not enough to satisfy Inanna. Her altar should contain beautiful items, but also those that symbolize strength and fierceness. A picture or statue of a lioness, her sacred animal, is essential.

In ancient images of Inanna, she carried a twisted knot of reeds representing fertility and abundance —so you might gather some reeds or vines and twist them into a knot or head-wreath. Weave in flowers if you wish. Fine jewelry, such as the lapis lazuli necklace she wore on her trip to the Underworld, is also associated with Inanna. Here are some suggestions for your altar. But as always, let your inner Goddess guide you!

At the Libra Moon, create an altar that's as aesthetically pleasing as possible. Go all out by buying your favorite flowers. Spritz yourself with a heavenly scent. Then consecrate the altar by lighting the incense and candles in Inanna's honor and calling her name. You might read her one of your favorite love poems to set the mood. Then tell her the secrets of your heart, and ask for her guidance— especially in regard to the Libra sector of your chart, if you know it.

You Will Need:

- 1 image of Inanna, perhaps with her consort Dumuzi
- 1 royal blue scarf or altar cloth
- 1 or 2 images or statues of a lioness
- 1 image of the planet Venus
- fresh flowers in a beautiful vase
- 2 pink candles
- 1 picture of you and your beloved
- some pomegranate seeds
- 1 book of love poems
- 1 lapis lazuli necklace, gold ring, or other fine jewelry
- attar of rose, or another you prefer

New Moon Ritual:
Cord-Cutting

The dark of the Moon is a time to banish what's unwanted in your life and plant seeds for the new. Because the Libra Moon is about relationships, it's time to review the ties that no longer serve you. Then you'll be cutting psychic cords to free your spirit. Because this can be an intense experience and you'll need time to assimilate the changes, it's best to cut only one person's cords during this ritual.

A psychic cord is an energetic bond between two people, also known as a hook. These hooks are quite real, even though you probably can't see them. They become embedded through physical means, such as sex, or through emotional means, such as love, anger, and dependency. In intimate relationships it's often both. But these hooks can also be planted in childhood by overbearing relatives, or through sexual abuse. They're often the source of obsessions, health issues, and creative blocks. If you frequently feel drained, sad, or angry, it's time to liberate yourself.

You Will Need:

- a quiet, private place
- your Inanna altar, if you've created one
- 1 black candle
- 1 silver knife
- 1 stick of sage for smudging
- a bathtub or shower
- Epsom salts and lavender oil
- your journal and a pen

1. Begin by determining whose cords you'll be cutting. Unless this person is extremely toxic, it doesn't mean you can never see them again—just that you'll no longer be adversely affected by their energy. It could be a person who is no longer alive, if you're having trouble moving on after their passing.

2. Once you're clear, stand in front of your Inanna altar or wherever you've placed your black candle. Light the candle and call upon Inanna and your own higher self to help cut the cords. Also call upon the other person's higher self. Pick up your silver knife. You can use an invisible blade instead, if you prefer.

3. Say aloud: "I now cut the cords that bind me to [person's name]." As you do this, slowly move your blade up and down your body while vividly imagining yourself cutting all energetic ties. Take care that you do not cut yourself in the process! Pay particular attention to your heart, solar plexus, and belly, because that's where most cords are attached. Also cut above your head and under your feet. You may actually feel the cords leaving. Either way, keep speaking the command aloud as you cut. If tears come, let them flow. If rage comes, give it a voice. Keep going until you feel complete.

4. Lay your knife down on your altar. Light the sage and smudge your entire body with it to clear your field. Breathe deeply, giving thanks to Inanna, your higher self, and the other person's. Blow out the candle (unless it's the glass-enclosed variety and you're letting it burn down).

5. Draw a bath and add lavender oil and Epsom salts. If you don't have a bathtub, a shower will do—just rub lavender oil on your body first. Then relax into the warm water. You're apt to feel a bit empty. To fill that space with new life, put your hands on your heart and infuse it with self-love, breathing deeply. Then put your hands on your belly and breathe strength into it. Get out when you're ready.

6. Before going to sleep, write in your journal about the experience. Be gentle with yourself over the next week or so; this process can bring up buried emotions. You might hear from the person whose cords you cut or have a dream about them. Send them healing energy and wish them well. It's time for you both to move on.

Full Moon Ritual:
Trance Dance

We are made of energy, and our energetic tendrils connect with everyone we come in contact with. As you learned in the section about the Libra New Moon, sometimes these energetic connections can hold us back. But in the right setting and with the right intention, they can also weave us together in primal unity.

To celebrate the connection-oriented Libra Full Moon, when the Sun is in energetic Aries, we'll be doing a Trance Dance—an ancient way of achieving oneness consciousness. The first time I did this ritual, I was amazed by the ecstatic experience of the collective trance state, and I never wanted it to end.

You Will Need:

- a group of like-minded friends
- a spacious, flat location, preferably outdoors
- comfortable walking shoes
- drummers or hypnotic music featuring drums
- healthy food and drink to share
- your journal and a pen

1. It's best to do this ritual at night under Luna's magical light. Wear comfortable shoes that are appropriate for the terrain. Form a circle, holding hands. Say a few words about Inanna and her magical lioness. Then let go and raise your arms. Say, "Hail and welcome Inanna!" Draw the lunar power down into your bodies for five minutes or so, until you feel fully charged.

2. Turn on the music or invite the drummers to begin a hypnotic rhythm. Walk slowly and deliberately in a random pattern, looking down and not making eye contact with one another. Focus your attention within. Weave in and out of each others' paths. Visualize yourself as a leaf carried by the cool autumn breeze letting your instincts and the music guide you. The pace may naturally pick up at some point. It will take thirty minutes to an hour to fully weave the web. You'll feel it when you're complete, as the pace will start to slow. Signal the drummers to wind down, or turn the music off.

3. Reconvene; go around the circle and share your experience. Raise your arms and say, "Hail and farewell, Inanna!" Hug each other, then feast to celebrate your sense of oneness.

4. Write in your journal before going to bed. Pay attention to any dreams or messages that may come in the following week.

When The Moon Is In Libra

Expect to be quite social when the Moon travels through this convivial sign, even if it's only behind closed doors. As an intelligent air sign, Libra favors everything that involves communication, creating and renewing unions and contracts, and bringing people together. This is a good time to schedule meetings, parties, and intimate rendezvous. Whether or not you're mated, love will be on your mind.

Create a mood for intimacy in your home when the Moon is in Libra by buying flowers with a pleasing scent that will waft subtly throughout the house. This is a good time to purchase a beautiful new outfit, sensuous sheets, or items to make your home lovelier. At the very least, be sure to give it a good cleaning and get rid of clutter to create more space, symbolically and literally, for love to enter. A serene home can create a romantic mood more quickly than anything else.

Because Libra is all about fairness and justice, you may find yourself having to mediate disagreements or build bridges between opposing factions during this time. This shouldn't be too hard if your Moon is in charming Libra. If it's not, you may have to deliberately hone your ability to listen carefully, be impartial, and detach yourself from the outcome. Let "the highest good for all concerned" be your watchword, no matter how frustrated you may get.

Also, especially if your Moon is in Libra, be aware that your authoritative tone could be perceived as cold, and that an inflexible stance can alienate others. There's a time and place for your fierceness—such as speaking out to right wrongs or to win justice for those who deserve it. And the Moon in Libra may give you a chance to do just that.

THINGS TO DO WHEN THE MOON IS IN LIBRA

Host or attend a gathering

Speak out for fairness and justice

Beautify your home

Have an intimate rendezvous with your beloved

Reaffirm your social ties and reconnect with friends

Go to court

Hold important meetings

Reach out to someone who needs your advice

Write an op-ed piece on something you believe in

Sign contracts (unless Mercury is in retrograde)

Do yoga to balance your body and mind

Have a heart-to-heart talk with your mate

Send flowers to someone you love (including yourself!)

Write love poems, stories, or songs

PART 10

Moon in Scorpio

Scorpio Moon women can be pretty intense. You possess great magnetism, along with the ability to see through people and cut to the chase. These are formidable assets, but they can also make others uneasy. Being in control makes you feel secure, and you're willing to take risks to attain it. When you were younger, you may have sought security through wealth, power, and passion. Yet you likely discovered that no matter how many goodies you acquired, there was still a deep fear of losing them. Over time, you learned that the only true security stems from self-awareness and trusting your deep connection to the feminine mysteries.

If your Moon is in Scorpio, your emotional nature is ruled by all-or-nothing Pluto. Passions reign supreme in your life. It's impossible to ignore them; the currents run too deep. You might seem sweet on the surface, but there's a powerful siren not far below.

Your Lunar Superpower

Your greatest strength is your undying passion. You will fight to the death for what you love, whether it's a person, project, or point of view. Your emotional strength is legendary. Some may be intimidated by the raw, direct power you bring to the table, but that doesn't make you any less awesome.

You're exceedingly loyal—once you trust someone. Scorpio often has trust issues. No doubt you've been betrayed before and are afraid of it happening again. You won't open up until you have certain assurances. But once you do, you're committed to the end.

Your Lunar Shadow

You can be quite hidden about your feelings and needs, which makes it hard for people to know you. This can lead to misunderstandings and distrust. Lack of forgiveness and a desire for revenge can also trip you up, as letting go is hard for you. Because your early home environment probably featured resentment or outright hostility, you may succumb to emotional dramas that have their roots in the past. Perhaps your mother tried hard to control you—and you've spent your life trying to break free. Your relationships will continue to reflect this pattern of control and rebellion until you transform it with awareness and forgiveness.

Your Sexual Nature

You're a primal Goddess in bed. You instinctively take your partner on a journey to the deepest mysteries. Spirituality and sexuality go hand-in-hand for you; you'd love exploring Tantric sex and learning to raise your ecstatic, snaky energy up your spine. You may need a bit of time to open up emotionally, but once you do, your passion is unequaled.

You're a powerhouse, but you tend to be "all or nothing." You can go for years having no sex at all, then plunge back in with unearthly vitality and stamina that leave the other person begging for mercy. You want to touch your partner's soul, and your intensity may scare those who aren't willing to go there. Watery Moons (Cancer, Scorpio, Pisces) can follow you into the deeper emotional realms. Earthy Moons (Taurus, Virgo, Capricorn) adore your passion and can bring you needed stability.

Your Karmic Path

You have the soul of a transformer. In other lifetimes, you were a priestess who used your sexual and emotional powers to heal and change lives. You may also have been overly protected by others. Perhaps you rarely left the temple and were bound by rules not of your own making. Seeds of rebellion were planted back then, and you vowed you'd never be controlled again. In this life you're determined to make your own way—and your own money—so you can shape your destiny.

Your big lesson this time around is to honor your feelings, no matter how dark. Whether in the temple or out in the world, you suffered painful losses in the past and still retain the memories deep inside—which can be a source of anger and depression. Sharing your feelings in a safe environment is essential for healing—whether it's in a trustworthy relationship or in therapy. Keeping secrets is no longer necessary.

SCORPIO MOON QUALITIES

Loyal

Passionate

Sexy

Secretive

Resilient

Possessive

Ambitious

Wealth-driven

Mysterious

Private

Resentful

Willful

Emotional

Perceptive

Soulful

Tenacious

Exacting

Scorpio Moon Women

Scorpio Moon women love a good mystery. You're attracted to the "dark side" of life, that which is hidden from ordinary view or shunned by the fearful or squeamish. The occult arts, such as astrology, Kabbalah, and tarot, intrigue you. You're probably not afraid of a little blood, either; many with your Moon sign are midwives or doctors—or at least enjoy watching gritty crime dramas.

Scorpio Moons love getting to the bottom of things. You'd make a great detective, psychologist, healer, or shaman. You're also good at managing people, finances, and businesses, though you may try to monopolize projects instead of delegating. You know your capabilities and may not trust others to do things as well.

Like the groundbreaking performer Isadora Duncan, whose sensual, scantily clad dance moves shocked Victorian audiences, you have an innate love and respect for the body and its passions. Yet sometimes it takes years (or a trauma) for your authentic self to surface. Another Scorpio Moon, Beyoncé Knowles, demolished her nice-girl image with the album *Lemonade*. She dug deep to get in touch with primal pain and indignation and transformed it into art.

Your Scorpio Moon can make you an excellent entrepreneur, manager, and self-made woman. Wealth and success come easily to you when you tap into your unique, indestructible inner Goddess. I know one Scorpio Moon realtor who consistently outperforms everyone else in the office. Another won acclaim by digging up dirt on Hollywood figures and writing books about them. Yet another puts her detective skills to work using cutting-edge techniques to diagnose and heal physical ailments.

Scorpio Moon blogger Ora North considers herself a spokeswoman for her generation, especially regarding sacred sexuality. In her essay, "Cry of the Millennial Witch," she writes, "[Our sexuality] is communication with the divine . . . a link between heaven and earth . . . It is a force all its own and won't be controlled or belittled." Her Scorpio Moon wants primal intensity, both sexually and spiritually. "We want our spirituality to taste like dark chocolate; deep, rich, a little bitter, a little sweet, sensual and complex. We want it real, we want it deep. We won't accept anything less."

Lilith's Sacred Animal: The Serpent

Ancient cultures revered the serpent; this mysterious, skin-shedding creature was worshiped as guardian of the mysteries of birth and death. High priestesses would keep snakes as familiars—sometimes twining around a sacred staff, as in ancient Crete, or slithering about the temple as protectors. Living in close proximity to the ground, the serpent would transmit the Earth Mama's messages to the priestesses.

Lilith took charge of her pleasure by undulating like a serpent while squatting atop a man. Jewish legends claim she had a human body from the waist up and a serpentine body from the waist down. The serpent is Lilith's sacred animal due to its Scorpionic ability to shed its skin and be reborn. Before orthodox religion took over, early Hebrews worshiped a phallic Serpent God as the consort of the Moon Goddess. They likened the snake to the penis—an equally mysterious creature that bestows infinite pleasure as it transmits the seed of life.

Immortality is said to be the special gift of the serpent; its sacred venom can kill as well as heal—or perhaps even bring the dead back to life. Snake venom has long been used to induce visions during sacred ceremonies. As a Scorpio Moon Goddess, you know the serpent's power; it undulates through you, body and soul. As you embrace your sexual birthright and offer it up to the Goddess, she will bring you new life.

Ancient Scorpio Moon Goddess: *Lilith*

Lilith is an ancient dark Moon Goddess so powerful that she was demonized by orthodox religions as a lustful sorceress and child-killing witch. She's the orgiastic part of the Mother Goddess that was cast into the wilderness long ago, surviving only in warped male fears of her sexual powers. Yet originally she was a symbol of all that was highest in a woman's nature, as embodied by her totem, the serpent.

Lilith is our sexy, sovereign Scorpio Moon Goddess. Like the other dark Goddesses, including the Hindu Kali, she can create and destroy at will. Scorpio rules the yoni, or gateway to the Underworld. From this sacred portal flows the "wise blood" that is the primal source of our power as women—but has for too long been shrouded in secret shame.

If you have Moon in Scorpio, your task is to redeem the dark Goddess Lilith and her serpentine powers by honoring your own hot, holy sexual nature and bodily functions—and perhaps helping other women do the same. Whether you're still menstruating or are past menopause and give your life blood in other ways, you can still embody Lilith's raw power.

It's easiest to tap into Lilith when the Moon is in Scorpio. But you can do it anytime you're feeling emotional or in need of understanding. Let's say your man forgot your birthday, and you're seething with hurt and rage. Light a candle to Lilith and call her name. Then put on some loud music and dance it out. Scream, moan, or cry. Your Scorpio Moon emotions have been repressed for too long—don't keep them in. Once you're feeling better, thank Lilith and give her a metaphoric high-five. Now you're ready to confront your clueless partner in a calmer way.

Creating an Altar to Lilith

Your altar to Lilith should be sumptuous and seductive. Start with a deep maroon cloth (ideally in velvet) to symbolize the blood of menstruation, childbirth, and death. Add a goblet of red wine and any of the items listed here that resonate with you—especially a bouquet of lilies if you can find them. Lilith's sacred flower, the lily, was once associated with the yoni. Because early Hebrews held that Lilith was formed from the same clay as Adam, making her his equal, be sure to include something fashioned of clay.

Drape the deep red cloth over the table or surface you're using as an altar, which should ideally be in your bedroom (the place of seduction). Spend some time arranging the elements until it feels right. Consecrate the altar by lighting the candles and calling Lilith's name. Ask her to bless and enhance your emotional and sexual power. Take a sip of wine and a bite of chocolate. Tell Lilith the secrets of your heart and ask for her blessing on anything you desire, especially if it's related to courage or sexuality. Visit Lilith's altar anytime you need emotional strength. You can ask for help in the Scorpio area of your chart, if you know where it is.

You Will Need:

- 1 maroon altar cloth
- 1 image of Lilith
- 1 image or statue of a snake and perhaps an owl
- 1 clay item, perhaps a bowl of water (Scorpio's element)
- 2 maroon candles
- 1 goblet of red wine and some dark chocolate
- ruby or garnet jewelry

New Moon Ritual:
Purification Rite

Salt and water are both cleansing agents. Any body of water, such as stream or deep lake is good for this ritual. However, the ocean is particularly purifying and regenerative, being a combination of the two. If you're able to take a walk on the beach before doing this ritual, please do so.

Known in pagan circles as the Witches' New Year, Samhain (All Hallows Eve) often falls near the Scorpio New Moon. This rite is uniquely suited for that time of death and rebirth, but it can also be practiced during periods of great stress, when you need to stay as clear-headed as possible, or when an obsessive pattern needs to be broken. Before you begin, give some thought to what old habit you're ready to release. This could be anything from denying your sexual needs by eating or drinking too much, to expressing your anger in ways that hurt others.

1. Fill your cup with water and stir in the salt. Pink Himalayan salt is especially healing, but ordinary table salt will do. Set the cup on your Lilith altar, if you've made one, or wherever you've placed your black candle. Light the candle and invoke Lilith to guide you. Say, "O Great Serpent Goddess, please help me banish fear and transform stress."

2. Sit with your chalice and close your eyes. Take three deep breaths into the bottom of your feet and up your body, grounding yourself. Bring to mind an image of whatever old habit is giving you the greatest difficulty right now. Formulate your frustration into a word or brief phrase and then open your eyes and speak or yell it into the saltwater. Imagine pulling the energy of darkness and frustration out of your heart and womb and then hurling it into the water with conviction. You may shed tears as you release the past. Let the saltwater absorb your fears and frustrations. Continue the process until you feel complete.

You Will Need:

- 1 beautiful cup or chalice
- pure water
- ½ cup (144 g) salt
- 1 spoon
- your Lilith altar
- 1 black candle
- 1 shovel or scooper to dig a hole
- 1 small quartz crystal
- bath and Epsom salts, optional
- your journal and a pen

3. Walk outside with your cup, scooper, and crystal and dig a small hole in the earth, perhaps near a favorite tree. Ask Lilith to transform the toxins in the water as you slowly pour it into the hole. Hold the crystal in your hands and blow into it, charging it with the power to transform your pain and help you move on. Put it in the hole and cover it with earth. Rest your hands on Mama Earth and thank Lilith for a fresh start.

4. Go back inside and wash your hands. Bid Lilith farewell and blow out the candle. It's nice to take a saltwater bath to complete the process.

5. Write in your journal about the experience. List several things you're going to change. For example, "I commit to blessing the day at my altar each morning" is a good replacement for your old habit of dreading each day as you awake. Or, "I commit to praising my husband for all he does right" effectively replaces your old habit of harping on him for what he gets wrong. It's best to not take on more than two things at a time to avoid getting overwhelmed. Be patient with yourself over the next few weeks as these new habits take hold.

Full Moon Ritual:
My Sexiest Experience

Now you'll be joining with like-minded sisters to stoke your fire and consecrate your sexual nature to the Goddess. Do this at night after the Moon has risen and you can hopefully see her clearly. The Sun is in earthy Taurus at the Scorpio Full Moon—a powerful combination for magic.

In this ritual, you'll be sharing an experience or a fantasy that stirs your blood. You can make it as graphic as you choose (or as everyone is comfortable with—discuss this ahead of time). The idea is to describe a moment that thrilled and/or turned you on. It may have occurred many years ago, or quite recently. It might have been a simple flirtation, or a full-on sexual encounter. You could read a short passage from an erotic novel if you'd rather not share a personal experience.

Before you begin, share what you've learned about Lilith so everyone can fully grasp what this hot Mama Goddess represents. And make sure everyone agrees to hold the shared experiences in strictest confidence.

Note: I don't usually recommend drinking wine during ritual, as it can blur the focus, but you may want to make an exception to help you relax (again, consult the group).

You Will Need:

- 1 or more trusted friends
- a safe place
- 1 athame (sacred knife) or crystal wand to use as a talking stick
- food and red wine for feasting
- your journal and a pen

1. Begin by going outdoors and raising your arms to the Scorpio Moon in her splendor. Even if she is obscured by clouds, salute her with "Hail and welcome, Lilith!" Draw her energy down into your bodies for at least five minutes, breathing in her radiance until you feel the power. You can remain outdoors if the weather is nice, or go back inside now.

2. Take the talking stick (knife or wand) to designate you have the floor, then share your hot experience. Make it come alive with sights, smells, tastes, and feelings. Humor is good! So are tears. Get it all out while your audience listens silently. When you feel complete, hand the talking stick to the next person, and repeat the process. Once everyone has shared, take a moment to close your eyes and feel how the room has altered.

3. Take your implement and go back outside. Hand it to another sister. She touches it lightly to your womb, saying, "I consecrate your sexual power in Lilith's holy name." Take a deep breath into your womb as she says the words, then release it slowly. Do the same for her. Repeat until everyone has been blessed. Then thank and release the Scorpio Moon. Each person raises her arms and says, "Hail and farewell, Lilith!"

4. Share food and wine and discuss your experience, including any new intentions you may feel inspired to make about your sex life.

5. Before bed, write in your journal. List your new intentions.

THINGS TO DO WHEN THE MOON IS IN SCORPIO

Research or make investments

Get your finances in order

Practice kundalini breathing

Have hot, steamy sex

Pay attention to dreams and insights

Visit someone in hospice

Go shopping for ruby or garnet jewelry

Eat dark chocolate and drink red wine

Read a sexy book, perhaps Anais Nin's Delta of Venus

Hold a confidential meeting or rendezvous

Share deep secrets with someone you trust

Get an astrology or tarot reading

Go to an underground club—if you dare!

When the Moon is in Scorpio

Scorpio Moon days can be emotional. There's a lot going on beneath the surface or behind the scenes that isn't immediately apparent. Sudden insights or hunches may arise, so watch carefully for them. Sex and power are on peoples' minds at this time of the month. Some may be plotting revenge, while others are writing enticing profiles to post on a dating site. Passions are running high—which can work in your favor with existing unions. Now is an excellent time to practice Tantric sex or kundalini yoga. But it's also easy to jump into new liaisons in the heat of the moment. It's not a bad idea to keep a low profile when the Moon is in Scorpio. Perhaps indulge your passions by watching a crime drama or reading a bodice-ripper.

Scorpio is associated with money, especially other people's money. Business-minded types will be planning mergers, holding confidential meetings, making big investments, or trying to fool the unaware—don't let that be you. It's a good time to get your finances in order, balance your checkbook, and research important purchases or investments before you commit to them. But if you're sure, this is a great day to make an offer or put your money down (unless the Moon is void).

Because Scorpio rules death and letting go, it's good to divest yourself now of old belongings—perhaps by having a yard sale. It may be time to end a relationship, or to grieve whatever or whoever is passing away. Scorpio is also associated with birth, so you may be celebrating a friend's new baby or the launching of a new business. The Scorpio Moon is particularly useful for making life-altering changes, such as a relocation or career change. Just check with your astrologer to make sure all the planets line up favorably.

PART 11

Moon in Sagittarius

Moon in Sagittarius makes you a big thinker, always exploring new spiritual or philosophical ways of seeing the world. Your emotional life is ruled by expansive Jupiter, so whatever you do, you do it in a big way. You're a "glass half full" person, unless something terrible has happened to sour your optimism. Even then, you'll persist in finding the meaning behind what happened. Spiritual growth is vital to you, and you seek to understand the cosmic laws that underlie all of creation.

An excellent teacher, you can also sell or effectively promote just about anything you believe in. You're success-oriented, and you love to tell stories about how you surmounted the odds. But you're also willing to make light of your foibles and follies to help others avoid doing the same. In fact, your great sense of humor is legendary.

Your Lunar Superpower

Your greatest strength is your generous spirit. You're always giving of yourself—whether it's your knowledge, contacts, or time. In fact, you're sometimes late to appointments because a conversation went longer than expected. Good luck comes naturally to you as you follow your instincts to chat up strangers and look for opportunities. Your fiery Moon makes you a stalwart champion of worthy causes, and once you get on your soapbox, it's hard to get you down.

Sagittarius is the sign of the Archer, eternally aiming to hit the mark. In olden days, when an archer failed to hit her mark, it was called a "sin." Obviously the word meant something quite different back then! Remember that you're always practicing at life, and that not hitting the mark is no real sin. Just pick up your bow and try again.

Your Lunar Shadow

Your downfall is being preachy or full of yourself. This can include posting way too much on social media, lecturing people on how to live their lives, and/or pontificating on "the truth" as you see it. Truth is very important to you, but you need to remember that there are many paths to the mountaintop. You can also burn yourself out by partying too hard or traveling too much. Make sure your home is a serene, grounding retreat with lots of green plants, scented candles, and beautiful objects, where you can recoup your energies before launching forth again.

Your Sexual Nature

You're an adventurer at heart, so your sexual experiences should take you on journeys and teach you new things. You enjoy having sex in out-of-the-way places, and there's nothing like a natural setting to get your juices flowing. You're passionate and fun, yet you need a long leash, as you're very independent. But your solo adventures reignite your spirit and keep the passion alive with your mate.

You're not too practical when it comes to love and can get involved before thinking it through. You're an open book, and you expect your mate to be the same. Avoid partners who are controlling or jealous. It could take you many years to feel ready for marriage. Some with this Moon sign would rather bond with dogs, cats, or horses. But a partner who listens to you and values your opinions can win your heart. The fiery Moons (Aries, Leo, Sagittarius) make great playmates and share your need for independence. The airy Moons (Gemini, Libra, Aquarius) will also delight you, and they're also usually pretty self-reliant.

Your Karmic Path

You have the soul of a master teacher. In past lives, you traveled from place to place, spreading knowledge and learning new things. You rarely stayed long in any spot; although everyone loved your bright spirit, inevitably you got itchy feet and moved on. You may have become a religious zealot, identifying so strongly with your beliefs that you tried to convert—or even destroy—those who disagreed. In this lifetime you are learning tolerance—to share your beliefs without alienating others. You're also learning to set boundaries rather than trying to be all things to all people. Resist the urge to move on when things get difficult.

Sagittarius Moon Women

My beloved Aunt Betty had Moon in Sagittarius. At twenty-three, she spontaneously married a handsome soldier she'd known for ten days before he was shipped off to war. Theirs was a great romance that spanned four decades. The life of a military wife, though difficult at times, suited my aunt's independent Moon. Moving from one state to the next, her restless nature never had a chance to feel boxed in. Along the way she developed a passion for painting, and once my cousins were grown she practiced her art while traveling to exotic locations.

If you share my aunt's Moon sign, I'm sure you could regale me with stories of your own grand adventures. You may have even garnered some fame for your over-the-top accomplishments. Like Sagittarius lifestyle mogul Martha Stewart, your knowledge and opinions make an impression on others. Perhaps you roam the globe sharing your talents like superstar singer Adele, or, like Yoko Ono, speak out for causes you hold dear.

Like the Sagittarius archer, you're always aiming for a goal—and your unbridled enthusiasm can get you there provided you have a solid plan. Otherwise you run the risk of being all talk and no action, or of burning out. You have the makings of greatness, along with the potential to be an inspirational figure if you follow a spiritual or creative path you love.

SAGITTARIUS MOON QUALITIES

Spontaneous

Adventurous

Travel-oriented

Truth-seeking

Spiritual or religious

Nature-loving

Independent

Light-hearted

Frank

Communicative

Energetic

Big thinker

Faith is the key to your success, and it can take you far. Your Moon sign often bestows artistic or musical talent. Having a trusted "witness" who sits down with you while you create or practice will help you master your art. I know Sagittarius Moon women who are gifted interior and clothing designers, hairstylists, photographers, writers, and healers, though it took some of them years before they believed in themselves enough to be successful. Don't let that happen to you. The world needs your contribution, even if it falls short of perfection.

Diana's Sacred Animal: The Dog

It's not clear when people first domesticated wolves and wild dogs to train them for hunting or keep them as pets, but they've been our faithful companions for centuries. Dogs are loving and fiercely protective, traits especially prized by women. As our boon companions, dogs (especially black dogs) came to be seen as witches' familiars—just like black cats.

Not all Sagittarius Moon women keep dogs, but those who do are intensely devoted to them. I know several who can't bear to be parted from their dogs and bring them wherever they go. One nearly lost her house after spending thousands of dollars on her ailing canine's care. Diana, whose hunting dogs were her family, might have done the same.

Dogs have long been associated with death. In ancient times, Diana's priestesses wore dog masks to pursue the Horned God (a man dressed as a stag). The spilling of his blood was intended to fertilize the land. As a spirit ally, the loyal dog helped the Goddess receive the dead and guide them safely through the Underworld.

Death also heralds new birth. The Tarot card for the Moon shows a dog and a wolf (the tame and wild aspects of the mind), howling at the Moon (emotions). Though often interpreted negatively, this card suggests that by using both intuition and logic, we can rise above fear into a higher dimension of oneness with Creation. If you have Moon in Sagittarius, your path is to unify wild and domestic, irrational and rational, into one passionate consciousness that uplifts the world.

At the Sagittarius Moon, why not take your dog (or borrow someone else's) for a long walk or a romp in nature? Or, visit a local dog park and watch the dogs cavort. This will awaken your inner canine, the part of you that remembers how to live wild and free. If you prefer, just tune in to your inner spirit dog and request whatever you need. If someone has recently passed away, ask your spirit dog to help them cross over safely.

Ancient Sagittarius Moon Goddess: *Diana*

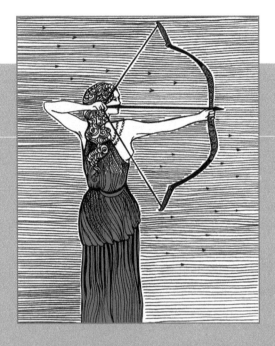

Imagine roaming an ancient forest at night by the light of a slender crescent Moon, your canine companions at your side. You stop for a drink at a spring, splash your face with cool water, and feel the Moon kissing your brow. Foxes and deer come out of hiding to join you. You speak each other's language, so there's no need for fear. This is your family; your heart expands with love for them.

Roman Goddess Diana (called Artemis by the Greeks) is the ultimate free spirit. A virgin Goddess—whole unto herself—Diana dwells in high mountains and lives by instinct. Symbolically, she has the power to help you track and recover your primal wisdom.

Like the Aries Moon's Hippolyta, Diana is a pagan Amazon Goddess. She embodies the fiery, independent Sagittarius Moon. More than just a Maiden Goddess, she was also worshiped as the Mother of All Creatures by early Latin tribes. She was the Nurturer, yet also the Huntress, killer of the very creatures she brought forth. Thus she represents the never-ending cycle of birth, death, and rebirth.

Worshipers adored Diana as reflected in tree branches or wooden logs—but sheaves of paper inscribed with knowledge are also her domain. The multi-breasted statue of Diana at Ephesus was etched with obscure phrases said to bring good luck when spoken aloud. Diana therefore represents the power of the written and spoken word, as well as the instinctive wisdom of nature.

Invoke Diana when the Moon is in Sagittarius, or if you need good luck with anything communication-related. Call her name before leaving on a trip; ask her to bless the journey and keep you safe. Request her inspiration before sitting down to write an important paper or book. When visiting a forested area or creek, call on Diana to renew your spirit. If your dog is lost, Diana can help you find him—just ask!

Creating an Altar to Diana

Although you could create one indoors, Diana's altar truly belongs outside. If you have a backyard or a patio, build your altar to this wild Goddess there. Create it near a tree if possible, in a sheltered spot to protect it from the elements. The bowl of water symbolizes Diana's sacred spring; you'll need to change it regularly.

Set up your altar on a day when the Moon is in Sagittarius. Arrange the elements in a pleasing but casual way. Of all the Goddesses, Diana is least concerned with aesthetics. Light the green candle and call her name to consecrate the altar. Flick some spring water onto your throat, center of communication, and third eye, center of insight. Ask Diana to help you see the big picture of your life, or to help you reach an important goal. Blow out the candle. Then take confident steps in that direction. If you know where Sagittarius falls in your chart, ask for help in that area of life.

You Will Need:

- greenery—plants or tree branches
- a bow and arrow, if you have them
- 1 image of Diana, preferably in statue form
- 1 statue of a hunting dog or forest animal, such as an owl or a deer
- 1 image or statue of a crescent Moon
- 1 green or brown altar cloth
- 1 green candle encased in glass
- 1 bowl of spring water

New Moon Ritual:
Tree Talk

Does it seem odd to have a conversation with a tree or a rock? The truth is that everything is alive and speaking to us all the time, if only we would listen. It's said that consciousness is entranced in rocks, sleeps in plants, dreams in animals, and awakens in humans. Native people have long sought guidance from the mineral kingdom. In an ancient Native American practice called "rock-seeing," a seeker would enter a wild place and walk until she found a rock that called to her, and then sit and ask a question, reading the rock's surface like a puzzle. Perhaps a sheep would appear, telling her to peacefully accept the situation at hand rather than fight against it. Or, the shape of a pregnant belly might suggest that the matter is still gestating.

You're welcome to try rock-seeing for yourself; I've had some real epiphanies that way, especially when visiting the red rocks of Sedona. If you travel to Hawaii, you can use volcano rocks, which also hold Sagittarius' element of fire. But because trees are sacred to Diana, we'll be consulting with them here.

You Will Need:

- your Diana altar
- 1 green, glass-enclosed candle
- a favorite tree, whether in your yard or a park
- a burning question
- an offering of water or milk
- your journal and a pen

1. If you've made an indoor altar to Diana, light the glass-enclosed green candle on it and ask for the Goddess's blessing on your ritual. Then go outside and stand in front of the tree you've chosen, bringing your offering of water or milk. (If your altar is outdoors, just light the candle there, making sure it is secure.)

2. Close your eyes and take three deep breaths up from your feet and exhale through your mouth, releasing all tension. Open your eyes and regard the tree. Soften your gaze and appreciate its beauty. Put your hand over your heart and feel your love for this kindred spirit until you sense the boundaries between you dissolving. You might want to put your arms around the tree or touch one of its branches.

3. Once you feel connected, pour the liquid at the foot of the tree and thank it for hearing your petition. Then speak your question aloud. Rather than posing a yes-or-no question, it's best to phrase it like this: "Please show me what this new job would be like for me." Or, "What is the best resolution to this issue with Joe?" Then let your eyes move slowly up and down the tree until you see an image in its bark that speaks to you. Pay attention to any associated feelings. Perhaps you see an anteater, which makes your stomach tighten up. This suggests that the job might involve a lot of nitpicky stress, including picking up after others. Or, perhaps you see a bird in flight, telling you to give Joe plenty of space. You may not see an image at all; you might just hear a voice in your head or get a feeling in your gut. Be receptive to whatever comes.

4. Once you've received your message, thank the tree and blow out the candle. Then write in your journal about what you received and what it meant. If you saw an image, you may also wish to sketch it out. Now create a New Moon intention related to what you'd like to manifest regarding the situation at hand. Write it down. Pay attention over the next two weeks for any guidance that may come.

Full Moon Ritual:
Enchanting Your Mind

The Sagittarius Full Moon opens the doorway to higher truth, and all we have to do is walk through and let our consciousness expand. And, because the Sagittarius Full Moon opposes the Gemini Sun, we've got both communication signs on our side.

Did you ever notice that "enchanting" contains the word chant? From the Latin word incanto, to enchant originally meant to weave a spell by making sounds in a repetitive manner. Chanting is magical; whether you're listening to music or making it yourself, the sound vibrations penetrate your body and go straight to your soul. Chanting induces a meditative or trance state, once considered fundamental to prayer. Gregorian chants are one example. They help us shift our minds and create new neural pathways to align on a deeper level with cosmic truth.

My favorite chants come from Deva Premal. Fueled by enduring love and the power of music, Deva and her husband Miten constantly travel the globe performing their rhythmic, meditative songs. My favorite is "A Deeper Light," their hypnotic collaboration with Maneesh de Moor. For this ritual, you might choose one of their recordings.

You'll be using the power of the Sagittarius Moon to magnetize whatever quality you most desire. So decide ahead of time what that might be. Do you most desire peace and calmness? Love and compassion? Prosperity and generosity of spirit? Health and healing? It's best to focus on mental states like these rather than specific things such as a new partner, tons of money, or a brand-new body. Why? Because Sagittarius rules the mind and spirit. And, you won't be able to manifest anything in a lasting form until you've first created the right mindset. The vibration has to match. This can be hard to swallow when you know that the right guy or a pile of cash would solve all your problems. But doing this ritual (perhaps repeatedly) will ultimately help you get there!

You Will Need:

- your Diana altar
- 1 pillow or chair to sit on
- 1 iPod, phone, or other music player loaded with hypnotic chants
- 1 small magnet
- your journal and a pen

1. As with the Sagittarius New Moon ritual, you'll be performing this one outdoors in Diana's natural element. Position your chair or pillow near your outdoor altar if you made one, within view of the rising Moon.

2. Lift your arms to Luna and salute her, saying "Hail and welcome, Diana!" Draw down her power for a few minutes, until you start to tingle. Then thank Diana for blessing the ritual.

3. Turn on your music and get comfortably situated. Take your magnet and hold it in your hand. Breathe deeply to ground and relax. Close your eyes and let the music take you on a journey. It helps to awaken the higher centers of your body if you chant or hum along softly. Let yourself disappear into the music. Continue for at least fifteen minutes, or however long it takes to feel the magic.

4. When you're ready, stand and lift the magnet to the Full Moon to charge it. Imagine Luna's illumination entering it and filling it with celestial power. Now draw that power into your cells, by slowly moving the magnet up and down your body. Charge yourself fully with whatever quality you're invoking (healing, love, etc.). Really concentrate on experiencing this. The energy may feel hot and tingly, or cool and calm.

5. When you feel complete, thank the Moon and say, "Hail and farewell, Diana!" Turn off the music and go back inside.

6. Write in your journal about what you experienced, including any revelations you had. Keep the charged magnet under your pillow at night so you can absorb its magic as you sleep.

When the Moon is in Sagittarius

Sagittarius Moon days are fun days, especially when they fall on a weekend. Now's the time to have an adventure, go on a trip, or at least visit a part of town you're unfamiliar with. If you have to work, try to liven things up a bit with humor and storytelling. Be generous to others; take someone out for coffee. Giving a talk, writing a paper, or doing research should go particularly well on these days.

This is a time for frankness and honesty (as long as you don't go overboard!). Have important conversations and truth-telling sessions now. Everyone will wax more long-winded than usual, though, so plan extra time between appointments. Some people like to schedule court dates for Moon in Sagittarius, a sign that, along with Libra, is associated with justice. If Sagittarius is your Moon sign, legal proceedings should go particularly well (barring any adverse aspects).

Because Sagittarius is one of the most spiritual signs, this is also a good time to consult oracles and do rituals for higher guidance, pray, or attend church. Most importantly, visit the sanctuary of nature—even if it's only for a stroll in the park or to water the plants and talk to the trees in your backyard. Your sense of faith will be strengthened by connecting with the natural world. Also, your higher, intuitive centers are acutely attuned to receiving spiritual guidance now, so pay attention to any dreams and hunches. If you've been feeling down, tell yourself an uplifting story about the wonder of your life—and watch things start to transform!

THINGS TO DO WHEN THE MOON IS IN SAGITTARIUS

Take a trip

Read (or write) a novel

Give generously to a cause

Enroll in a class

Find a mentor

Have a truth-telling session

Throw a last-minute party

Buy a lottery ticket

Talk to trees

Visit the library

Adopt a dog (or take yours on a long walk)

Get your car fixed or detailed

Pursue your art

Help a friend out

Chat up strangers

Go on a long drive or day trip

Write down your dreams and hunches

PART 12

Moon in Capricorn

Those with Capricorn Moon can be tricky to figure out. There is something undeniably shrewd and capable about you, yet you're not always easy to know emotionally. Most of you are warm, witty, and fun to be around, always there for others and willing to get the job done. Yet there can also be a steely or calculating edge to you. It all depends on your relationship to Saturn, which rules your emotions and early life. If a strict parent expected the impossible or withheld affection, your lunar nature may be more cautious and reserved than warm and accepting. But either way, your inner fortitude is impressive.

In other words, you have grit. Reese Witherspoon's Oscar-winning role as June Carter Cash in Walk the Line is a good example. The actor found her "vein of gold" as Johnny Cash's long-suffering but indomitable wife. Interestingly, both Witherspoon and Carter Cash have Moon in Capricorn!

Your Lunar Superpower

Your greatest strength is your determination to accomplish your goals. Capricorn is associated with the goat, an agile creature that perseveres up the mountaintop. Many Capricorn Moons do find their way to the top, becoming CEOs or business owners. Meaningful work is essential to you; you thrive on being useful and productive. Even if you're not working in the world, you apply your competence and organizational skills to running a tight ship at home. You aim toward nothing less than self-mastery—and often get there, especially later in life. You age well and come into your own as you mature.

You're a natural authority figure and a protective mama with your kids. As a boss or manager, you have clear boundaries and realistic expectations of others. You tend to be hard, however, on those who slack off (including yourself!).

Your Lunar Shadow

Inflexibility is your challenge. A rigid attitude can even lead to spinal or joint issues such as arthritis, a classic Capricorn ailment. Emotionally, being too stiff or cold could alienate others and plunge you into dark moods or depression. Learning to accept your emotions, both dark and light, is essential to your happiness. Some with your Moon sign are married to their work and okay being without a partner. Although your traditional nature respects the institution of marriage, you also like to protect your interests. It's smart to maintain your own bank account when married.

Your Sexual Nature

Your earthy nature gives you a strong sexuality. But youaren't apt to jump into bed with someone unless you really feel connected. Once you warm up and relax, you're quite lusty. You love to laugh and tease the other person. The older you get, the sexier you become. It's not always easy for you to express your feelings, though, and you may be shy about trying new things in bed. But once you master a skill, watch out!

In relationships, you're often a late bloomer. You need a nurturing mate, even a "house husband" who tends the hearth while you're out making your mark on the world. You can go the long haul once you know your partner is committed to you. Earthy Moons (Taurus, Virgo, Capricorn) are commitment-oriented; they understand your reserve and are willing to take their time and let things develop. Watery Moons (Cancer, Scorpio, Pisces) stir your passions and help you relax into your feelings.

Your Karmic Path

You have the soul of a builder. In past lives, you loved to bring tangible things into form—such as homes, businesses, and bank accounts. Yet you also put duty ahead of everything else. Perhaps you had heavy family responsibilities or needed to work very hard to survive. You may have become a workaholic or an alcoholic, numbing yourself to feelings you couldn't face. In this life you're learning to loosen up and enjoy life. Spending quality time with family and sharing feelings with those you love is new karmic territory for you. Make it your priority. As long as you avoid sliding back into old patterns of toughing it out alone, your sense of discipline will help you master the work-life balance you crave.

Capricorn Moon Women

Moon in Capricorn women mean business—you do what it takes to make things happen. I know women with your Moon sign who've owned import shops, managed nonprofits, worked as paramedics, and run schools and insurance agencies. Even if you're a healer or an artist, you probably operate your business efficiently. One Capricorn Moon friend started an expressive arts studio that's become the neighborhood hangout—she gets to be in charge and host cool events, as well as socialize with folks who love art as much as she does. She worked long and hard to achieve this dream, however—and to keep it up and running!

Many remarkable women have the Moon in enduring Saturn's sign. Known as the "Empress of Fashion," style arbiter Diana Vreeland ruled the fashion world for decades. When Cher first strode onto the scene, she rocked everybody's world with her powerful voice and glamorous image. And she didn't put up with husband Sonny's attempts to control her for long. Capricorn Moons can't stand being under someone else's thumb. Although you will defer to authority figures you respect, you'd rather be the one others look up to. In fact, you need to be respected in order to feel secure.

You have high standards, often cracking the whip to achieve your goals. And, you take no crap from anyone. Yet you're not as tough as you may seem. You're actually quite sensitive, though you may try to hide it with an "I don't care" attitude. But woe to anyone who underestimates you! Ditzy Capricorn

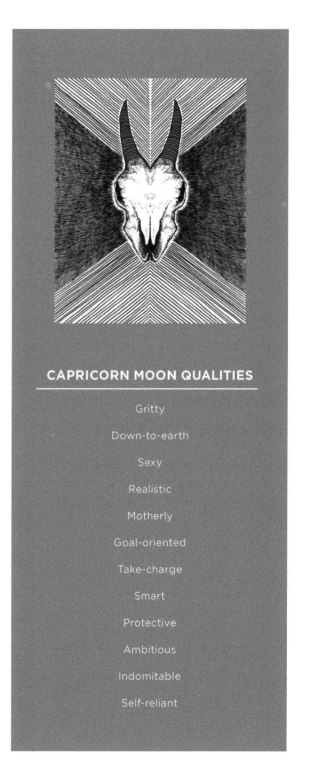

CAPRICORN MOON QUALITIES

Gritty

Down-to-earth

Sexy

Realistic

Motherly

Goal-oriented

Take-charge

Smart

Protective

Ambitious

Indomitable

Self-reliant

Moon comedian Lucille Ball was the brains behind the wildly popular *I Love Lucy* show. The first woman to head a TV production company, Ball bought out Desi Arnaz's share after their divorce and went on to create her own empire.

If you also have a big dream, you don't have to hide your true nature to pursue it. Spiritual teacher and change-agent Marianne Williamson, author of *A Return to Love*, ran for Congress a while back. Although she didn't win, she definitely broadened the political discourse—and says she learned a lesson about speaking her truth rather than doubting her instincts and waiting for someone else to tell her what to do. As she told Oprah Winfrey in an interview for Oprah's Super Soul Sunday on July 29, 2012, the experience "taught me what I should have already known: to only listen to myself."

Amaltheia's Sacred Animal: The Goat

Despite its association with the baser side of life, the goat is a loving, friendly creature. Extremely intelligent, curious, and stubborn, it has long been a symbol of fertility and healing. Capricorn's goat horn symbol is said to mirror the crescent Moon, while the goat herself was often linked to Moon priestesses who inhabited mountain shrines in ancient times and practiced their healing arts.

Because Zeus was suckled by the goat nymph Amaltheia, goatskin was revered by the ancient Greeks and often made into water pouches or drum heads. A goatskin shield was the aegis, or ultimate protection, and the goat's horn became a cornucopia of plenty. Able to nimbly climb mountain peaks and presumably see the past, present, and future, the goat was worshiped by many cultures and came to symbolize the indomitable spirit of Capricorn.

The randy goat (especially in masculine form) was also associated with ancient fertility festivals. So when the Church began to stamp out matriarchal ways, the goat was maligned. The Old Testament called it lewd and dirty. Later, Christians went even further, transforming the innocent goat into the Devil incarnate.

It's time we started giving the goat the respect it deserves, especially in its female form as the sacred, generative power of women. Honoring Amaltheia in the rituals that follow will help reawaken your primal goat power. In the meantime, find a local dairy where you can buy goat milk, and maybe play with the goats while you're at it! I met a goat named Elsa recently at a local organic farm. She was so loving and friendly that my spirits were uplifted for hours afterward. If a meet-and-greet isn't possible, check out one of those darling YouTube videos of baby goats hopping around. Your earthy, playful life force will be stoked to the max!

Ancient Capricorn Moon Goddess: *Amaltheia*

Our Capricorn Moon Goddess may not seem very tough, but she exemplifies the inner fortitude your Moon sign is known for. In Greek myth, Amaltheia was a goat-nymph who hid the infant Zeus in a cave, saving him from his murderous father Cronus. As the child's foster mother, she protected him at great risk to herself, suckling him at her breast until he was old enough to stand on his own.

The nymph called on her warrior buddies to aid her in defeating Cronus. But rather than provoking a bloody battle, she had them dance, shout, and clash their spears and shields so Cronus couldn't hear the baby's crying. Symbolically, she called forth her warrior nature to protect the divine child. This is something many Capricorn Moon women need to learn— to shield themselves from a harsh parent (or a harsh world) by nurturing and protecting their inner divine child.

As an earthy goat Goddess, Amaltheia is a sexual being. Yet unlike her brother, promiscuous Pan, she tempered her passions in service to her foster child. She is our Capricorn Moon Goddess for her indomitable nature, patience in waiting out the danger, and willingness to temporarily put her own needs aside for a higher purpose. She represents the self-mastery to which all Capricorn Moons aspire.

Amaltheia's myth paints a portrait of a protective and loving parent who's also willing to let her child go—something many Capricorn Moon women find hard to do. Whether it's an actual child, a marriage, a job, or a phase of life, moving on becomes easier as you nurture your Moon with self-love and acceptance.

You can invoke Amaltheia when the Moon is in Capricorn, at the Winter Solstice when the Sun enters Capricorn, or at the Capricorn New and Full Moons. Light a candle to her and ask for her help with any tough decisions you're facing. Also turn to her when you feel the need for comfort or protection. Amaltheia can be the nurturing mom you never had; drink a cup of goat milk in her honor and feel its nourishment.

Creating an Altar to Amaltheia

To honor the goat nymph within yourself, you'll be creating an altar to both your inner and outer selves—your sensual passions as well as the goals you want to achieve. Then you'll call on Amaltheia's help to nurture and protect what's most vulnerable within you, which will make you strong enough to climb any mountain. Amaltheia's colors are those of nature—moss green, butter yellow, sky blue, brick red. So find a cloth in one or more of those colors for your altar and then add symbols such as the ones that follow. Even a few of them should be enough to inspire you!

When the Moon is in Capricorn, set up your altar in a part of your home that reflects your personal and professional goals. In feng shui, that's the area around your front door, inside or out. But anywhere that feels right to you is fine. Light your brick-colored candle and call Amaltheia's name to consecrate the altar. Offer her a tiny cup of goat milk to symbolize the nurturing of your inner and outer selves. Ask for her help with achieving a goal. If you know where Capricorn falls in your chart, focus on that area of life. Write down your goal and put it on the altar, giving thanks.

You Will Need:

- 1 altar cloth in nature-inspired colors
- 1 statue or an image of a goat or goat nymph
- 1 protective symbol, such as a knife, spear, or shield
- 1 small cup of goat milk
- 1 brick-colored candle
- 1 symbol of a goal you're attempting to reach
- 1 small goatskin drum, if you have one
- 1 cornucopia filled with fruit
- 1 brick or piece of one

New Moon Ritual:
Sacred Commitment

Capricorn is an unbelievably grounded, even heavy, energy. (Think of the huge fixed mountains where Capricorn's native animal, the goat, resides.) I learned this the hard way when I tried to raise energy through a Cone of Power (see next chapter) at a Capricorn New Moon ritual years ago. The Cone refused to take off, no matter how hard we tried. It was a humbling lesson (appropriate for Capricorn) in working with the energy at hand, rather than trying to make it into something it's not.

So why not maximize this pragmatic Capricorn New Moon, by making (or renewing) a sacred commitment to something that's vital to your well-being? This could be anything from a healthy body or bank account to a relationship that's working for both of you. We all have good intentions, but sometimes life gets in the way and we forget to follow through on them. Then the weight creeps back on, the savings account gets depleted, or you forget to spend quality time with your mate. Before the ritual, take time deciding on one thing you're willing to commit to, something that's so sacred you'll do anything to make it happen.

You Will Need:

- brick-red nail polish
- 4 red bricks
- a stick of sage, a shell or bowl, and matches
- 1 brick-colored candle, on your Amaltheia altar if you've made one
- citrus-scented oil, such as lemon or grapefruit
- 1 statue of a goat, if possible, or 1 reddish stone or a crystal
- a clear goal or outcome
- your journal and a pen

1. To get yourself in the mood before the ritual, paint your toenails brick red (or have it professionally done). Putting this Capricorn color on your toes will help remind you of your commitment. Once your nails are dry, place a brick in each of the four main corners of your home or office. This grounds the energy and creates sacred space. Then light your sage and walk clockwise through each room, seeing the smoke purify and burn away any negativity. This is especially important if there has been any recent drama or heaviness in the space. Pay particular attention to the corners, where stale energy collects. Breathe deeply as you walk, releasing any stress or anxiety.

2. When you're done, put out the sage on the shell or bowl. Anoint the candle (on your altar if you've made one) with citrus oil and deeply inhale the crisp, cleansing fragrance. Light the candle and center yourself by gazing into the flame. Ask Amaltheia to bless you with her brave, nurturing energy. If you have a statue of a goat, anoint it with the oil and appoint it your talisman whose job it is to remind you of your commitment. Or, you can anoint something else as your talisman, such as a reddish stone or crystal.

3. Hold your talisman in both hands and think about the commitment you're about to make. Visualize your highest outcome—such as you looking great in a bikini, a specific amount in your savings account, or you and your partner renewing your vows. Declare your intent out loud, speaking directly to your talisman. Say, "I give thanks that (my desired outcome) is already in place. I commit to (joining a weight loss group, saving 10 percent of my paycheck each month, having two date nights a week.)" Kiss your talisman and ask it to help you follow through.

4. Blow out the candle and journal about the experience.

5. Follow through on any actions you committed to taking. Join that club and go to the meetings. Write a reminder on your calendar to deposit money in your savings when your check arrives, then do it. Schedule that romantic cruise with your mate and don't let anything get in the way of it happening. If you should break your commitment, don't beat yourself up for it. It takes practice to establish any habit. Just relight your candle, re-anoint your talisman, and speak your commitment again. Do this as often as you need to. Leave the bricks in the corners of your space, at least through your Capricorn Full Moon ritual. If you like how they make you feel, you can leave them there permanently.

Full Moon Ritual:
Self-Nourishment

The Sun is in nurturing Cancer at the Capricorn Full Moon. This is the mother-father axis, which challenges us to balance love and caring with boundaries and protection. If you've suffered a wound that involves lack of nurturing, as many of us have, this is your opportunity to begin or deepen the healing process by working with the lunar right brain. In this ritual, you'll be re-enacting the Amaltheia myth, giving yourself the nourishment you needed when you were younger and creating effective boundaries to protect you from further harm or misunderstanding. If you found a doll to represent your inner child at the Cancer New Moon, invite her to join you for this process. Or use a favorite stuffed animal as your child surrogate.

You Will Need:

- a private place where you won't be disturbed
- your Amaltheia altar
- 1 brick-colored candle and citrus oil
- 1 rattle, drum, or other noise-making device • 1 doll or stuffed animal to cuddle
- 1 cup (235 ml) or baby bottle of goat milk
- a view of the Full Moon, if possible
- your journal and a pen

1. Light the candle on your Amaltheia altar and anoint it with citrus oil, just as you did for the Capricorn New Moon ritual. Inhale the scent deeply as you call on the Goddess to protect you during your ritual. If the Full Moon is up, go outside and salute her, saying "Hail and welcome Amaltheia!" Draw down her power for a few moments and feel it charge your cells with courage and determination.

2. Then go back inside and take your noise-makers in hand—even a spoon and pan will do. Or just clap your hands vigorously. Walk around your room or house (or outside, if you don't mind disturbing the neighbors), shouting and making noise, as if to scare away intruders. In the myth, this is how the warriors protected baby Zeus so his predatory father would not hear his cries. Be like those warriors, protecting your vulnerable inner self. Imagine a protective veil of sound surrounding you. Do this for ten or fifteen minutes, or until you feel complete.

3. Then sit with your doll or stuffed animal and talk to her, telling her she is safe. Ask her if there's anything she needs. Have a dialogue with her and make sure she feels heard. Feel your feelings, let them out. Then drink the goat milk, feeling nourished. Rest in the knowledge that it's now safe to fully be yourself, and to let others in. Blow out the candle.

4. Go back outside and salute the Moon, saying "Hail and farewell Amaltheia!" Feel gratitude as you bathe in her radiance. Then go back inside and write in your journal about what came up for you. You can repeat this ritual whenever you feel the need for strength and comfort.

When the Moon is in Capricorn

Capricorn Moons are great for focus and concentration. Capricorn favors tackling tasks you might not ordinarily be up for (such as organizing your closet or preparing your tax returns) and having tough conversations you've been putting off. However, slow and steady wins the race. Take your time with whatever you do, whether it's clearing your inbox or hiking a mountain, and do it properly.

Because Capricorn rules age and authority, now is the time to plan for retirement, sit down with your boss or financial planner, and visit your ailing grandma. Take good care of your own aching bones and stay limber with a yoga class or a chiropractic adjustment. We all tend to feel a little creaky when the Moon is in Saturn's sign; a massage helps work out the kinks.

Because Capricorn is a take-charge cardinal sign (it initiates the season of winter), this is a good time to begin new work or health-related projects. Weight loss and fitness regimens stand a fighting chance if begun under Moon in Capricorn; your willpower will be stronger than usual. Capricorn is also a sign that loves to build, so any renovations or home-based building projects begun now should go well (unless Mercury is retrograde or the Moon is void—check your daily guide).

Capricorn rules the knees, which are associated not only with flexibility but also the willingness to humble yourself to a higher power (i.e., getting down on your knees to pray). Clear insight rarely comes when you're tense, so first go for a long run or dance and shout to release any frustrations. Maybe a good cry is in order. Only then will you be truly receptive to the wisdom of your inner authority. Sit with any issue that's troubling you and ask your higher self for insight. Then pay attention to your gut feelings for guidance.

PART 13

Moon in Aquarius

Moon in Aquarius people are quirky and open-minded. You're accepting of all and most definitely ahead of your time. Aquarius is an air sign, so you have a fine mind and good communication skills, and you can make rapid-fire connections between things. Some think Aquarius is a water sign because it's known as the water-bearer. But the fluid that your Moon pours forth is more like nectar from heaven—spiritual sustenance for thirsty souls.

With such an honest, uplifting emotional nature, you're a natural spiritual guide and healer. You may also be gifted at seeing the future; you're probably already living there! But you can also feel alienated when it becomes obvious the rest of the world hasn't caught up with you yet. It's up to you to find your tribe—other farsighted folks who get your message of peace, love, and equality.

Your Lunar Superpower

Your greatest strength is your open, friendly approach. Everyone wants to have you on their team. You're so even-keeled and inclusive that most people like you, and your sunny smile ultimately wins over anyone who doesn't. Sometimes you might seem a little remote or testy, but that's just because you've retreated to your inner world and need to be left alone for a while. Yet when one of your many friends calls on you for help, you're always there for them.

You may be a bit eccentric, but you're also brilliant. Aquarius is ruled by change-agent Uranus; you love to stir up a little trouble, and to bring together like-minded people for the purpose of sharing revolutionary ideas. And if you should join forces with another Aquarius Moon, together you'll become the hub around which a galaxy of people orbits.

Having the Moon in the sign of revolution doesn't guarantee your ideas will be progressive. Sarah Palin has an Aquarius Moon. She's definitely quirky, but her conservative ideas are more Saturn than Uranus. Saturn ruled Aquarius until Uranus was discovered at the dawn of the Industrial Age, and some Aquarian types harken back to Saturn's old-school ways.

Your Lunar Shadow

Fear of emotional involvement can hold you back. You learned self-sufficiency early on, and feel most comfortable when others give you lots of breathing room. You may also fear losing your freedom if you get too close. Because you are so easygoing, though, you may not realize how much independence you

need until you're already entangled. Then you may end up withdrawing into your head or the Web, becoming crazy busy or throwing yourself into causes to avoid a partner who wants more than you can give. If, however, you get the emotional freedom you need—plus a strong, open friendship—you'll be an incredibly loyal partner.

Your Sexual Nature

Yours is an experimental Moon sign, so you're always up for trying new things sexually. You may even be quite kinky, especially if your curiosity is aroused. You're also super fun and friendly, but your partner may find you a little remote emotionally, due to your intense need for freedom. You tend to intellectualize your feelings; lovemaking helps ground you in your body and bring out your emotions. In fact, you'd love to explore feelings with the right person, and experiment with Goddess worship.

Because you're a bit androgynous, you can easily play the male or female role. The airy Moons (Gemini, Libra, Aquarius) are your intellectual match and are capable of giving you the freedom you need. The fiery Moons (Aries, Leo, Sagittarius) will stir your spirit, open your heart, and accompany you on exciting sexual journeys.

Your Karmic Path

You have the soul of a visionary. In previous lives, you devoted yourself to rallying people around an inspiring ideal. But, when so many needed your encouragement, you may not have gotten around to honoring your needs or achieving your personal dreams. Perhaps you were a scientist or an astrologer who lived a life of the mind, and often retreated to your "ivory tower" to solve problems for others. Or, you may have been so involved with groups that you failed to shine as an individual. In this life, you're learning to stop hiding your light under a bushel and step out as the unique person that you are. Start by getting in touch with your deepest personal desires and make them your priority. Then use your visioning skills to make them come true, and get the support you need.

Aquarius Moon Women

My Aquarius Moon cousin recently moved to a small Arizona town, where she's been attending Bible study classes. I was surprised to hear this, since she's never been religious. She says she likes the community, but there's more to it than that. The minister (her brother-in-law) lets her lob incendiary verbal grenades into the discussions, because they always liven things up. My cousin may shock conservative folks with her out-of-the-box questions, but she also gets them thinking.

In the 1960s, Aquarius Moon photographer Diane Arbus shocked people as well. She pulled back a curtain to reveal a world most had never seen, turning her lens on dwarfs, giants, transgender people, nudists, and circus performers. Her groundbreaking work paved the way for more ultra-realistic photography. Your Aquarius Moon, being so experimental, may also be attracted to the kinky side of life. The line between male and female can be blurred for your Moon sign, which champions brotherly (and sisterly) love and equality between the sexes.

Your Aquarius Moon's androgynous flair can also make you downright sexy. Some of our savviest young supermodels, such as Cara Delevingne and Gigi Hadid, have Moon in Aquarius, giving them a tomboyish charm and friendly, carefree sensuality (plus impressive Instagram accounts!). Most Aquarius Moons have tons of friends of both sexes, though some just have one bestie who'll last until the end. If you're lucky enough to have such a pal, you'll treat her like gold, as true friendship is the Holy Grail for you.

Soaring through the skies above the Earth, birds have long symbolized freedom. Bird-headed goddesses feature prominently in many creation myths, representing rebirth and resurrection. Ancient pictographs show strange, godlike beings with bird heads, likely symbolizing the evolution of human consciousness and our connection to divine, otherworldly realms. Eagles and hawks symbolize power and farsightedness in indigenous cultures. Shamans would dress in cloaks made from bird feathers and "fly" to other realms to seek guidance and healing.

Though many birds can inspire and uplift us, we have a special relationship with the twittering songbirds who share our gardens and homes. They brighten our lives and remind us to lighten up. Rhiannon's blackbirds were powerful familiars for the Faerie Queen. As masters of the element of air, signifying communication, they relayed messages to her from other realms.

The ancient Druids saw blackbirds as magical beings; their sweet music was said to lull the sick or wounded to sleep and heal them at the soul level. These birds were also considered emissaries to the

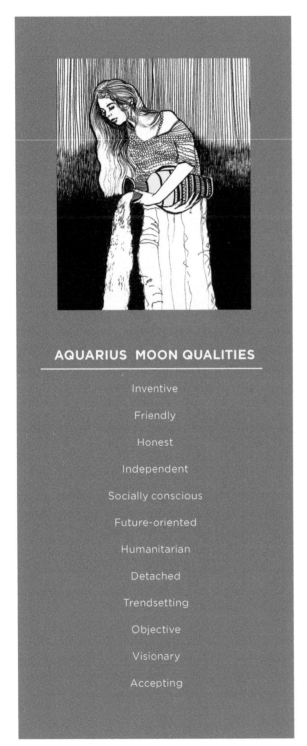

AQUARIUS MOON QUALITIES

Inventive

Friendly

Honest

Independent

Socially conscious

Future-oriented

Humanitarian

Detached

Trendsetting

Objective

Visionary

Accepting

Otherworld who helped carry deceased spirits aloft and on to their next home. Shamans would often eat the blackbird's favorite food, rowan berries, to ease their waking minds to sleep and charge their psychic abilities prior to journeying to other realms.

If you have Moon in Aquarius, you may feel a strong connection with the bird nation. Whether you keep parakeets, feed hummingbirds, or simply enjoy listening to songbirds chirping outside your window, the feathered clan has a message for you. Allow them to guide you to greater self-acceptance and sense of community. When the Moon is in Aquarius, set out a feeder or scatter some seeds for them. Sit for a while and listen to their soothing sounds, and listen for any wisdom they may impart.

Ancient Aquarius Moon Goddess: *Rhiannon*

Rhiannon was the Queen of Faeries immortalized in Welsh legends. A sovereign Goddess of the Moon and wind, she epitomizes the independent Aquarius Moon woman. Rhiannon appeared to the mortal King Pwyll (Paul) as a beautiful, dreamlike vision in a golden gown, riding a glowing white horse, her blackbird familiars circling around her.

Pwyll was enchanted by the beautiful young Goddess and she with him, but like most Aquarius Moon women, Rhiannon was hesitant to give up her freedom. Ultimately, though, she took her beloved to her father's crystal castle in the faerie realm. After using her powerful magic to banish a persistent suitor, Rhiannon married her true love and returned with him to the mortal world.

All was well until Rhiannon bore a son, then found herself punished for his disappearance and alleged death. Even her treasured husband turned on her. Yet as Rhiannon grieved for her former life, she matured into a Death Goddess who was able to help others transition. It was said that her guardian blackbirds sang so sweetly that the dying went gladly to their deaths. Then the winds of change blew once more. Rhiannon's missing son reappeared. She was absolved, forgave those who had misjudged her, and rejoined the living.

The Aquarius Moon woman must often descend from a heady, idealistic realm to a realistic earthly one, or at least learn to balance the two. If you've suffered great losses, try to cultivate hope like Rhiannon did—it's Aquarius's greatest blessing. If you need Rhiannon's help with cultivating hope or balance, call her name when the Moon is in Aquarius. Eat some fresh rowan berries (or blackberries) to awaken her energies within, especially if you've suffered a recent loss and are trying to regain your sunny disposition—the hallmark of an Aquarius Moon temperament.

Rhiannon's Sacred Animal: The Blackbird

Soaring through the skies above the Earth, birds have long symbolized freedom. Bird-headed goddesses feature prominently in many creation myths, representing rebirth and resurrection. Ancient pictographs show strange, godlike beings with bird heads, likely symbolizing the evolution of human consciousness and our connection to divine, otherworldly realms. Eagles and hawks symbolize power and farsightedness in indigenous cultures. Shamans would dress in cloaks made from bird feathers and "fly" to other realms to seek guidance and healing.

Though many birds can inspire and uplift us, we have a special relationship with the twittering songbirds who share our gardens and homes. They brighten our lives and remind us to lighten up. Rhiannon's blackbirds were powerful familiars for the Faerie Queen. As masters of the element of air, signifying communication, they relayed messages to her from other realms.

The ancient Druids saw blackbirds as magical beings; their sweet music was said to lull the sick or wounded to sleep and heal them at the soul level. These birds were also considered emissaries to the Otherworld who helped carry deceased spirits aloft and on to their next home. Shamans would often eat the blackbird's favorite food, rowan berries, to ease their waking minds to sleep and charge their psychic abilities prior to journeying to other realms.

If you have Moon in Aquarius, you may feel a strong connection with the bird nation. Whether you keep parakeets, feed hummingbirds, or simply enjoy listening to songbirds chirping outside your window, the feathered clan has a message for you. Allow them to guide you to greater self-acceptance and sense of community. When the Moon is in Aquarius, set out a feeder or scatter some seeds for them. Sit for a while and listen to their soothing sounds, and listen for any wisdom they may impart.

Creating an Altar to Rhiannon

Rhiannon is a magical nature Goddess. Your altar should reflect her otherworldly beauty, which emanates from the faerie realm. You'll need an image or statue of a faerie and/or a blackbird, her sacred creature. You might also want to include her trusty steed, a white horse. Your altar should contain some metallic gold or silver to reflect Rhiannon's queenly status. Because wind is her magical element, you could include a wind chime, fan, or anything else that stirs the air. Include a small bowl of earth for grounding. And be sure to honor Rhiannon's death aspect as well, with a picture or memento of someone or something you've lost.

Rhiannon's altar should be in plain sight; no dark corners for this airy Moon Goddess. Choose a location near an open window, if possible. At the Aquarius Moon, drape your shimmery fabric over a table or other surface, then add the other elements in a pleasing way. Cleanse and consecrate the altar with your aromatherapy spritzer. Then call Rhiannon's name and ask her to guide you—especially in the area of your chart occupied by Aquarius, if you know it.

You Will Need:

- diaphanous fabrics with metallic touches
- 1 image of Rhiannon
- 1 picture, carving, or statue of a blackbird
- some rowan berries (or blackberries)
- 1 small bowl of earth
- 1 statue or picture of a white horse, if you choose
- 1 wind element, such as a wind chime
- 2 gold or silver candles
- 1 picture or emblem of who or what you've lost
- 1 aromatherapy spritzer with a fragrance you love

New Moon Ritual:
Circle of Acceptance

For those of us in the Northern Hemisphere, the Aquarius New Moon falls at a particularly frigid time of year, with spring only barely on the horizon. It's easy to feel alone or excluded at this time. So in this ritual you'll be calling on the spiritual sustenance of Aquarius to light a spark of nurturing and acceptance—from yourself or others. Aquarius is associated with visualization, imagination, and the creation of a desired outcome that can shift your reality.

Here you'll be drawing on the warmth and light of multiple candles to create a magical circle of power that will manifest the sense of inclusion you desire. That can include a new circle of friends, greater acceptance by certain people, a sense of being surrounded by spiritual guides, or the feeling that you're no longer alone.

Choose the area in which you'll be creating your magic circle with care. It's best to do it in a room where you regularly do (or intend to do) rituals, as this New Moon ceremony will define and deepen your sacred space.

You Will Need:

- your Rhiannon altar
- 1 handful of rowan berries or blackberries
- 1 aromatherapy spritzer with a fresh scent
- uplifting music (I love Moon Fever by Air)
- 1 clear quartz crystal
- at least 4 white pillar candles (8 if you prefer)
- an intention related to acceptance
- your journal and a pen

1. Light the candle on your Rhiannon altar, and ask the Goddess and her blackbirds for a blessing on your ritual. Place the cluster of berries on the altar as an offering. Spritz yourself with the aromatherapy spray and breathe in the heavenly scent. Place your right hand on your heart and center yourself. Root your feet firmly to the ground. Turn on the music.

2. Put your crystal near the center of the sacred circle you'll be creating. Then place an unlit candle in the east, south, west, and north, moving in a clockwise direction. If you're using extra candles, position them in between the others. Light each one in turn, going clockwise from east to north.

3. Now sit in the center of the circle. Place your crystal between your hands and take some deep breaths. Feel the warmth of the flames surrounding you. Allow the light to fill your being and your crystal. You are now between the worlds, a place where magic can happen.

4. It's time to use your Goddess-given power of visualization to generate the acceptance you desire. Perhaps you long to be accepted into a like-minded circle of spiritual sisters, or a new workplace where you feel more at home. Create a clear image in your mind's eye and feel the sense of camaraderie in your heart and soul. Or, perhaps it's self-acceptance you need. You might imagine yourself walking into a gathering, dressed in an outfit that makes you look and feel dynamic. If you can't come up with an image, ask Rhiannon for help and go with whatever arises—even if it makes no sense to your conscious mind. Keep focusing on the image for at least five minutes or until it starts to feel real.

5. Once the image is fixed, lift the crystal to your lips and say something like, "Beautiful crystal filled with light, this task I bid you expedite. Bring acceptance unto me; as I will, so shall it be." Repeat this three times with conviction. Sit with the magic for a while. Then blow out each of the candles in reverse—from north to west, south, and east. Thank the directions for blessing your intentions.

6. Place the crystal on your altar and leave the circle. Thank Rhiannon for guiding you, and eat her sacred berries to assimilate her power and stimulate your dreams. Write in your journal about the experience. Then watch for intuitive promptings, such as someone to contact, a group to join, or an invitation to accept.

Full Moon Ritual:
Cone of Power

The Cone of Power is a tried-and-true method of raising energy in ritual magic. It's particularly effective at the Aquarius Full Moon, when the Sun in open-hearted Leo opposes the Moon in visionary Aquarius. Worshipers stand in a circle and slowly move their hands in a clockwise direction, picking up speed—until at last they raise their arms up and release the energy to the heavens.

No matter how many times I participate in a Cone of Power, the moment of send-off never fails to thrill me. In the Dragon Sister Circle to which I belong, we often conclude our rituals in this way. It's a powerful way to send the magic we've just done to the Goddess, who can then use it to manifest our intentions.

In this ritual, you'll be joining with like-minded sisters to manifest a shared goal. It's best to meet in the evening when Luna is most likely to be visible.

You Will Need:

- at least 3 like-minded sisters
- a place of power, preferably outdoors
- a shared intention
- 1 crystal for each person
- food and drink to share
- your journal and a pen

1. Sit in a circle and take turns sharing what's up for each of you. This will determine what intention you want to send forth. If everyone is distressed about a tragic event that just occurred, you might send healing energies to the victims. If one of your sisters needs a new home, you could dedicate the Cone of Power to her. Or, if you're all in a financial crunch, focus on manifesting new work or a specific amount of cash.

2. Once you're ready, go outside with your crystals and form a circle. Speak a few words about Rhiannon and her totem blackbirds. Then everyone raise their arms and say, "Hail and welcome, Rhiannon!" Draw in the lunar power for a few minutes, until you're brimming with incandescent light. Then state your intention out loud.

3. Join hands for a moment in reverent silence. Then drop them and slowly begin moving your hands in a wide, clockwise circle, synchronizing with your sisters. Hum softly, increasing in volume as your hands move faster and lift higher. Don't rush this; the Cone of Power should take five to ten minutes to build. When it's reached a peak, you'll know it. At that point, fling your hands skyward as you release your intention with joyful, triumphant whoops and hollers.

4. Kiss your crystals; they now contain the power of this ritual. Hug each other and celebrate by feasting. Before going to bed, write about the experience in your journal. Keep track of any manifestations over the next few weeks.

When The Moon Is In Aquarius

Aquarius is about social connections and heightened communication. When the Moon travels through this high-frequency sign, you might find yourself a bit frazzled. You may be prompted to contact old friends, go to networking events, or join a Meetup group. The phone will likely be buzzing with invitations and appointments.

Although Aquarius does emphasize community, it's also associated with the individual self. So it's a good time to treat yourself to a spa day, write in your journal, create a vision board to manifest a goal, or volunteer for a worthy cause just because it makes you feel good. Work-wise, Aquarius favors all things technological, such as building or improving your website, sending out mailings or resumes, researching new careers, and putting together a cutting-edge team.

Aquarius is a bit rebellious, so you may feel an urge to make a break with the past. Take care, however, not to cut your losses too soon, or to plunge into new things before you've fully investigated them. There's a certain excitement in the air right now, but it's wise to consider what's in your best interest to avoid getting overextended or charging off in the wrong direction. Consulting an expert is a good idea now. Inventive solutions may arrive out of the blue, but brainstorming is also an excellent route to problem-solving.

Because Aquarius rules all that's new and progressive, you may have a vision for the future or a sudden flash of understanding. Most of all, follow your heart's desire and unique path, regardless of what anyone else thinks.

If you have Moon in Aquarius, you may seem especially overextended or eccentric to others now. Sit on the Earth to keep yourself grounded and realistic.

PART 14

Moon in Pisces

If you have Moon in Pisces, the mystical, creative realm is your true home. Your psychic functions are highly developed; you sense other people's feelings and thoughts, and you may even perceive invisible beings or receive messages from the other side. Even if you shut these abilities down long ago, they still exist just beneath the surface. You may experience them more in dreams than in waking life.

You are a sensitive soul and need to honor your deep feelings and promptings. You may walk into a club or other gathering place and feel your skin start to crawl. That's your intuition telling you to get out, or at least to purify yourself later with an Epsom salt bath. Just because no one else could sense the yucky vibes doesn't mean they didn't exist. Your psychic radar will also alert you to dead-end relationships and people who don't have your best interests at heart.

Your Lunar Superpower

Your greatest strength is your imagination. You swim in a sea of art, poetry, beauty, and music. Others can become intoxicated by your magical allure, which stems from your uncanny access to the dreamy, right-brain lunar hemisphere.

A diehard romantic, you believe in true love and are willing to hold out for it. Your partner needs to worship you, and you'll reward him with undying devotion. You need someone grounded and stable, however, as you can easily get carried away by your feelings and imagine the worst. If you truly love someone, you'll write him poems and sacrifice a great deal to keep him happy. Just make sure he deserves your devotion!

Your Lunar Shadow

Your downfall is playing the victim. Since facing reality isn't your strongest suit, you can sometimes fool yourself into thinking people (or God) are out to get you and start to feel sorry for yourself. Your potent imagination can conjure up threats where they don't exist, or at least exaggerate them greatly. Better to use it for manifesting the good.

Another aspect of your lunar shadow involves your strong emotions. Since Pisces is connected to the sea, with its storms, fog, and unknown depths, your emotional weather can quickly turn dark if you are angered or stressed. I've seen Pisces Moon women fly into a rage that no one saw coming. It's good to be honest about what you're feeling, but don't let it build up until you explode and cause serious damage.

Your Sexual Nature

Yours is the most romantic Moon sign of all, and you'll shower your beloved with adoration or even put him or her on a pedestal. Worshiping the God (or Goddess) in your partner comes naturally to you, with your dreamy, spiritual nature. Just make sure that the other person is genuine, as you tend to fall for fantasies or those who aren't what they appear to be. You need a partner who can hold a strong container for you, honor your sensitivities, and journey with you to emotional realms. Being in or around water arouses you, whether it's a hot tub or moonlight dip in a lake. Watery Moons (Cancer, Scorpio, Pisces) are your emotional equal and can dive to the depths with you. Earthy Moons (Taurus, Virgo, Capricorn) love your mystical gifts and can help ground you.

Your Karmic Path

You have the soul of a mystic. In previous lives, you were a dreamer who brought magic to many people. Yet you may not have possessed the clarity or practicality to make your dreams real. You wanted to make a difference in the world, but you often got derailed. Perhaps you succumbed to fantasies, trusted the wrong people, or fooled yourself into thinking all was well when it wasn't. Now you're learning to read the fine print and be honest with yourself and others. Dedicating yourself to a cause such as human or animal rights can give you a sense of purpose. Be realistic with your expectations, but don't give up on your dreams.

Pisces Moon Women

The Pisces Moon woman has a certain glamour. Like French designer Coco Chanel, whose Pisces Moon gave her an elegant, instinctive sense of style, you stand out from the crowd. And you can work magic with next to nothing. I once knew a Pisces Moon woman with little money but great taste. She managed to transform even the shabbiest abode into a mystical, inviting temple with artfully draped scarves, wall hangings, and other thrift store treasures.

You're a magical chameleon with a deep inner life. People sense this—they can see it in your eyes—and are magnetically drawn to you. They can also drain you, though, and you need to take periodic retreats to get back in touch with your own soul. Some Pisces Moon people lead tragic lives, but they're also able to turn their pain into art. One thing is certain: Whether happy, sad, or in between, you have the ability to touch people at a level much deeper than words, and to leave a lasting impression.

You may be drawn to a creative field, such as acting or design, or perhaps you'd rather help and heal. Many medical professionals have Moon in Pisces. Christiane Northrup, M.D., a top authority on women's health and wellness, uses her Pisces Moon to address our mind, body, emotions, and spirit in a way few doctors have done. Her book *Goddesses Never Age* breaks new ground for older women, teaching us how to stay sexy and vital into our sixties and beyond.

One older Pisces Moon friend stays sexy and vital by dressing in sparkly outfits—like the costume she designed for a mermaid parade. One sunny day, six senior women came together on a Southern California boardwalk to fulfill a dream by inviting their inner mermaids out to play. The crafty sirens strutted their sassy selves in glittery costumes to the sounds of "Yellow Submarine." My friend says they were welcomed like rock stars, as men whistled and women cheered. She doesn't know if her mermaid pals share her Moon in Pisces, but they're clearly passionate about the undersea realm that Pisces rules!

You're apt to feel a kinship not only with the sea, but also the Moon. Perhaps you intuitively sense that she won't leave you alone in darkness. A writer friend who was born at a Pisces Full Moon told me that she tends to wax poetic—and also, at times, melancholy. But she says that the Moon's reflective light helps her understand her inherent nature. She has learned to find strength in her sensitivity and to see her Pisces Moon as a dependable flashlight that illuminates the darkest parts of her life.

Sedna's Sacred Animal: The Seal

In northern lands such as Scotland and Scandinavia, seals are associated with the deep feminine soul and the Underworld. The mournful, oddly human cry of the seal can be both stirring and frightening. This call from the sea may remind us of our origins in the salty waters of our mother's womb, or of the oneness with creation that we once had and lost. The seal's song also urges us to stay open to our unconscious minds, from which our deepest dreams and longings arise.

Sedna and her seal companions were worshiped in various guises by the indigenous people of the north, especially the British Isles. Some Irish families even claim to be descended from the union of humans

PISCES MOON QUALITIES

Poetic

Dreamy

Imaginative

Sensitive

Perceptive

Unrealistic

Unpredictable

Psychic

Self-sacrificing

Visionary

Addiction-prone

Compassionate

and seals. As beautifully depicted in the movie *The Secret of Roan Inish*, certain female seals, known as selchies, were said to emerge every hundred years from the sea to take a human mate. They would cast off their seal skins to conceive children who, like them, could move between the worlds. Eventually the siren call of the sea would prove too strong, and the selchie would return to her oceanic family. But she still provided for her human children by leaving fish for them to eat.

If you have Moon in Pisces, you're like the selchie— navigating back and forth from your watery emotional depths to everyday reality. And with each visit to the undersea realm, you return with creative gifts that bless the world around you.

You can invoke Sedna's totem animal when the Moon is in Pisces by visiting a local beach or even taking a trip to a wild northern land. Toss some flowers into the sea as an offering. If that's not possible, call upon your spirit seal by creating an altar to Sedna, making sure to include an image of a seal and/or a mermaid. Watch *The Secret of Roan Inish* to really get in the mood. If you can find a recording of seal songs, play it while you gaze at your totem animal and ask it for a personal message.

Ancient Pisces Moon Goddess: *Sedna*

In the native Inuit culture of the Arctic, survival in the frozen tundra was based on man's relationship to the animal kingdom. The Inuit followed strict protocols for hunting and eating, to honor the animal spirits—especially those of the ocean.

Sedna was their Goddess of the Sea. In one version of her myth, she was originally a beautiful young woman who, unhappy with the suitors her father had provided, married a dog instead. Her father threw her into the sea and chopped off her fingers as she tried to climb back into the kayak. Angry and despondent, Sedna sunk to the bottom and grew a fish tail. Her severed fingers became the creatures that inhabit the sea. Soon she came to love her family of seals, walruses, dolphins, and fish.

Sedna means "Big Bad Woman" in the Inuit language. The fishermen were afraid of this emotional, unpredictable Goddess, who sometimes brought storms and giant waves. They did rituals in her honor to ensure she would keep providing them with food.

Because Pisces rules the ocean, with its connection to the unconscious mind, women with Moon in Pisces have direct access to the depths—with all their treasures and terrors. Your Pisces Moon is badass. So claim your gifts and greatness, your anger and regrets—as well as your ability to forgive and move on. You have a great deal to offer us all.

You can invoke Sedna when the Moon is in Pisces, or at the New or Full Moons in that sign. Sedna knows your suffering. Call her name when you need comfort, or when you're angry about the indignities of life. If you know where Pisces falls in your chart, ask for help in that area of life. Imagine Sedna's salty, healing waters washing you clean.

Creating an Altar to Sedna

As an undersea Goddess, Sedna loves oceanic treasures. So create your altar in the deep blues and greens of the sea, adding shells, saltwater, and images of the ocean creatures Sedna loves, to make her feel at home.

If you've always had a thing for mermaids (and you probably have, if you're born at a Pisces Moon), then this is your chance to display your collection. Sedna, with her fish tail, was the original mermaid. Include images or statues of her familiars—seals, walruses, dolphins, whales, and fish. Fish netting can be a nice addition, perhaps draped above the altar with shells attached. If you keep fish, such as goldfish, add them to the altar. Living creatures are powerful magic!

It would be nice to set up your Sedna altar in the bathroom, near your tub so you can gaze at it while bathing. But anywhere that feels right will do. At the Pisces Moon, arrange the elements as artfully as possible. Like you, Sedna is a sensitive soul and feels best surrounded by beauty. Consecrate your altar by dipping your fingers into the salty water and touching them to your heart and belly. You can ask Sedna to help you in the area of life occupied by Pisces in your chart, if you know it.

You Will Need:

- 1 beautiful bowl full of seawater (or salted water)
- gossamer ocean-colored fabric or netting
- 1 mirror (which corresponds to the element of water)
- images of ocean creatures
- 1 image of a dog, if you choose (Sedna's loyal mate)
- 1 bowl of goldfish, if you have them

New Moon Ritual:
Dreaming Candle

Dreams are the ultimate Pisces experience. As we navigate the oceanic dream world at night, we throw out psychic nets and catch symbolic clues about our existence. Yet few of us recall our dreams, let alone pay much attention to them. When the Sun and Moon embrace in the watery depths of Pisces at the New Moon, it's a perfect time to cultivate your dream life—by collaging a magical candle guided by your subconscious desires.

Collage is my favorite medium. Anyone can do it, even if you think you have no artistic ability. In my New Moon Collage classes, people regularly astound me with their gorgeous, evocative creations. Usually we collage onto poster board, but for this ritual you'll be pasting images onto a tall, glass-enclosed candle. Any color will do; you can find them at most grocery stores.

You'll also need to collect magazine images that inspire you. Or, you can search websites such as

You Will Need:

- a collection of images
- 1 tall glass-enclosed candle
- glue sticks
- scissors
- lavender oil
- your Sedna altar, if you've made one
- your favorite hypnotic music
- your journal and a pen

Google Images or Pinterest for inspiration or use your own pictures (copy them first or they won't stick). Wiccan priestess Devra Gregory saves the Goddess images from her WeMoon calendars for collaging candles at power times. You can join with others and pool your images for this ritual, or do it privately. Set aside several hours, ideally in the evening, as you don't want to feel rushed.

1. Find a comfortable, well-lit table and assemble your materials. Turn on your hypnotic music. Close your eyes and ground yourself, taking a few deep breaths. Ask Sedna to bless your ritual and send inspiration. You might have a particular intention for your collage, such as improved health, financial flow, or a more open heart. But it can be even more powerful just to let your subconscious mind take over and guide you to what your soul desires.

2. Let your Dreaming Mind choose how the images want to be cut up and combined on the candle. You might use one or two—or a dozen. There is no right way to do this; follow your intuition. Once you've glued your images down and the candle feels complete, place it on your Sedna altar and light it. Turn up the music (or put on something more stimulating) and raise some energy by dancing. Send your desires up with the flame. The taller candles burn for a week, continually dispersing your wishes.

3. Then take a ritual bath with lavender oil, soaking in the New Moon magic. Afterward, sprinkle a few drops of the oil onto your pillow to stimulate your dreams. You might want to drink some herbal tea or even a small amount of wine before bed. Write in your journal about the experience, and about any intentions you came up with. Then, as you slide into the undersea world, intend that you'll remember any important dreams. If you wake during the night from a dream, write it down or you might not remember it. Your Pisces New Moon dreams are capable of giving you potent subconscious guidance; pay close attention to them.

Full Moon Ritual:
Intuitive Reading

Like the other water element signs, Scorpio and Cancer, Pisces is highly sensitive and intuitive. I once attended a women's gathering in which we took turns "reading" for each other. No one considered herself psychic, yet we all tuned in on each other's inner lives in ways that surprised, even shocked, us. We are all born with psychic abilities, but in many cases these faculties shut down when authority figures condemn or ridicule us for knowing things we couldn't possibly have known. If you have Moon in Pisces, your psychic powers are stronger than most, but the Pisces Full Moon can bring them out in anyone who sincerely applies herself.

Trusting your instincts is the key to success with this process. You may have no idea why you're getting an image of a roaring lion while gazing at a gentle sister, but the image will mean something to her. She might be angry at someone, and your image could help give her the courage to stand up for herself. It's good to have at least four of you participating in the circle; they can be total strangers or sisters you know well. Be sure to meet in the evening when Luna is visible outside. If you live near the beach, it would be extra special to gather next to the waves.

You Will Need:

- at least 3 like-minded sisters
- a comfortable place to circle, inside or outside
- 1 stick of sage
- food and drink to share afterward
- your journal and a pen

1. After everyone has arrived for the ritual, go outside and form a circle. Smudge each sister with sage. Take three deep breaths to get centered. The Sun is in earthy Virgo at the Pisces Full Moon, which will help ground your heightened perceptions.

2. Say a few words about Sedna and her totem seals. Next, raise your arms and salute the Moon, saying, "Hail and welcome, Sedna!" Draw her power into your bodies. Then everyone speaks the command: "Open wide my psychic gates; bring messages to which I can relate. Bless me with the power to see; as I will, so shall it be."

3. Sit comfortably and begin with the first recipient. One by one, each sister shares whatever comes to her while gazing at the recipient in a soft, unfocused way. Go with the first image, phrase, or impression that arises. The recipient remains silent until everyone has spoken, then she shares her experience. Go around the circle until everyone's had a turn.

4. Go back outside and thank the Moon, raising your arms and saying, "Hail and farewell, Sedna!" Now it's time for feasting.

5. After everyone leaves, write in your journal about the experience.

When The Moon Is In Pisces

Pisces Moon days are dreamy and emotional. You may feel quite creative, but your imagination can also run away with you. Getting lost in fantasies can be fun—like watching a stirring movie. But try to keep your feet on the ground when it comes to important decisions such as making big purchases or choosing a new partner.

You'll be feeling extra sensitive on these days, so if your feelings get hurt, try not to stifle them. If you push the pain aside, it's apt to fester and erupt in self-blame or lashing out at others. Your psychic powers are heightened now, especially if you have Moon in Pisces. Pay attention to your dreams, and any intuitive promptings. If you have a hunch about someone, it's probably accurate. If you feel guided to take a different route to work, follow your internal guidance—it could keep you safe.

Pisces rules joyful feelings such as happiness and unconditional love, so it may be easier than usual to embrace pleasure, forgive others, or open your heart to those you care for. Mystical states and awareness of subtle energies will sharpen your perceptions and enhance your spiritual powers. This is an excellent time to do rituals, meditate, take a timeout, or purify yourself in a sweat lodge or sauna.

Beware of defeatist attitudes, and do your best to accept others as they are. Everyone is reflecting back to you an aspect of yourself, which you can learn from. If your cat won't stop harassing you for food, take a look at your own eating habits. Pay attention to deep feelings seeking an outlet. Succumbing to addictions and procrastination is easy to do at this Moon.

Call on Sedna for help if you're feeling lost, and give yourself plenty of downtime to recover from stress. Like Sedna and the selchies, enjoy your undersea journey!

THINGS TO DO WHEN
THE MOON IS IN PISCES

Write down your dreams and
contemplate them

Work on creative projects

Have a romantic date with your beloved

Make music, paint, or dance

Go into seclusion

Forgive someone

Go swimming in the ocean,
or collect shells

Buy new shoes (Pisces rules the feet)

Write poetry

Clean out your closets

Avoid potentially toxic locations

Go to an AA or Al-Anon meeting

Attend a meditation group or church

Take an acting or dance class

Turn your bedroom into
an inviting temple

Catch up on sleep

Visit a friend in the hospital

Confess your feelings

Get a healing treatment

Have a good cry

Questions for Reflection and Journaling

1. What are you most scared of right now? Feel into the root of the fear. Is it real, or just a vague imagining?

2. Is it easy or hard for you to relax and trust life, knowing you are protected? How might you develop a stronger connection to your Higher Power?

3. Do you sacrifice yourself too much for others, or tend to play the victim or martyr? How might you communicate your needs and let other people support you?

4. Do you remember your dreams and write them down? If so, interpret a recent dream. If not, commit to remembering them.

5. Are you expressing your innate glamour and mystical qualities? If not, is there something that's keeping you from doing so?

6. Are you a fool for love, falling into romantic fantasies? Write down the top ten feeling qualities you must have in a relationship.

7. Do you hold yourself (and others) to impossibly high standards? Where do you think that tendency comes from, and how might you relax it?

8. Is there something in your life that feels like a burden? Are there habits or patterns that leave you feeling drained or overwhelmed?

9. Do you dance enough? Put on your favorite music and let yourself go.

10. Are you comfortable with your psychic, intuitive knowing? Do you trust it?

It's been such a joy to journey with you on this priestess path, and I hope you're inspired to keep on walking it. Please remember that your true power comes from your inner Goddess and her representative, the Moon. Being willing to express your gut feelings and sacred sexuality is what makes you a Goddess—both within yourself and in the world.

I'll leave you with something inspired by Florence Scovel Shinn, an early-twentieth-century writer who loved spiritual affirmations. To strengthen your resolve each morning, repeat the following words at your altar:

"Now the waters of my Red Sea part, and I walk forward into my Promised Land. Miracle shall follow miracle, and wonders shall never cease."

Recommended Reading

The Mists of Avalon, Marion Zimmer Bradley

The Artist's Way, Julia Cameron

The Vein of Gold: A Journey to Your Creative Heart, Julia Cameron

The Druid Animal Oracle, Philip and Stephanie Carr-Gomm

Making the Gods Work for You, Caroline Casey

Being a Lunar Type in a Solar World, Donna Cunningham

Dear Lover: A Woman's Guide to Enjoying Love's Deepest Bliss, David Deida

The Red Tent, Anita Diamant

The Chalice and the Blade, Riane Eisler

Women Who Run with the Wolves, Clarissa Pinkola Estes

The Book of the Moon, Steven Forrest

Moon Magic, Dion Fortune

The Sea Priestess, Dion Fortune

Mysteries of the Dark Moon, Demetra George

Lessons in Astrology as Magic, Dana Gerhardt

Big Magic: Creative Living Beyond Fear, Elizabeth Gilbert

Mythic Astrology, Ariel Guttman and Kenneth Johnson

Woman's Mysteries, Ancient and Modern, M. Esther Harding

In Praise of Slowness: Challenging the Cult of Speed, Carl Honoré

The Wizard of Us, Jean Houston

Astrological Transits, April Elliott Kent

The Essential Guide to Practical Astrology, April Elliott Kent

The Magdalen Manuscript, Tom Kenyon and Judi Sion

Lunaception, Louise Lacey

Care of the Soul, Thomas Moore

Everyday Moon Magic, Dorothy Morrison

Delta of Venus, Anais Nin

Goddesses Never Age, Christiane Northrup, M.D.

The Mysteries of Isis, deTraci Regula

The Game of Life for Women and How to Play It, Florence Scovel Shinn

Ritual, Power, Healing and Community, Malidoma Some

New Moon Astrology, Jan Spiller

The Spiral Dance, Starhawk

My Stroke of Insight, Jill Bolte Taylor

Jambalaya, Luisah Teish

Mama Gena's Owner's and Operator's Guide to Men, Regena Thomashauer

Mama Gena's School of Womanly Arts, Regena Thomashauer

Pussy: A Reclamation, Regena Thomashauer

The Women's Encyclopedia of Myths and Secrets, Barbara G. Walker

A Return to Love, Marianne Williamson

Websites for Teachers Featured in this Book

Julia Cameron: www.juliacameronlive.com

Donna Cunningham: www.skywriter.wordpress.com

Clarissa Pinkola Estes: www.clarissapinkolaestes.com

Dana Gerhardt: www.mooncircles.com

Elizabeth Gilbert: www.elizabethgilbert.com

Devra Gregory: www.sacredflamefirecircle.com

Jean Houston: www.jeanhouston.com

April Elliott Kent: www.bigskyastrology.com

Tom Kenyon: www.tomkenyon.com

Ora North: www.oranorth.com

Christiane Northrup: www.drnorthrup.com

Lisa Schrader: www.awakeningshakti.com

Linda Savage: www.goddesstherapy.com

Luisah Teish: www.yeyeluisahteish.com

Regena Thomashauer: www.mamagenas.com

Siobhán Wilcox: www.siobhanwilcox.com

About the Author

Simone Butler has been a professional astrologer and Moon worshiper for more than thirty years. She has written many forecasts for Starscroll and www.Tarot.com. Based in San Diego, Simone does astrology consultations and blogs bimonthly at her website, www.astroalchemy.com. Her first book was Astro Feng Shui: Making Magic in Your Home and Life.

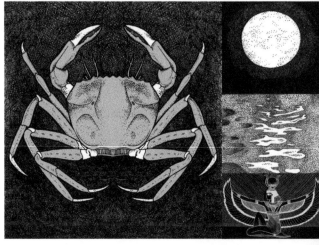

Index

A

Aliens, 10

Altars

to Amaltheia, 124

basic facts about, 5

to Diana, 113

to Hippolyta, 30

to Inanna, 93

to Isis, 61

to Lakshmi, 41

to Lilith, 103

to Oshun, 72

to Rhiannon, 135

to Scheherazade, 51

to Sedna, 144

to Vesta, 84

Amaltheia, 122–124

Ancient cultures, 9–10

Andrews, Edson J., 13

Aquarius

activities for when Moon is in, 139

characteristics, 131–132

greatest strength and weakness, 130

karmic path, 130–131

Rhiannon, sacred goddess, 133–135

rituals, 136–138

sexual nature, 130

Aries

activities for when Moon is in, 35

characteristics, 27–28

greatest strength and weakness, 26

Hippolyta, ancient goddess, 28–30

karmic path, 26

rituals, 31–34

sexual nature, 26

B

Behavior and phase of Moon, 10–11

Blood Moon, 11

C

Cameron, Julia, 7

Cancer

activities for when Moon is in, 66

characteristics, 58–59

greatest strength and weakness, 57

Isis, ancient goddess, 59–61

karmic path, 57–58

rituals, 62–65

sexual nature, 57

Capricorn

activities for when Moon is in, 128

Amaltheia, ancient goddess, 122–124

characteristics, 121–122

greatest strength and weakness, 120

karmic path, 120–121

rituals, 125–127

sexual nature, 120

Cunningham, Donna, 9

D

Diana, 111–113

E

Eclipses, 11

Egyptian cosmology, 25–26

Ereshkigal, 92

Estes, Clarissa Pinkola, 49

F

Ficino, Marsilio, 8

Fortune, Dion, 26

G

Geb and Nut, 25

Gemini

activities for when Moon is in, 55

characteristics, 48–49

greatest strength and weakness, 47

karmic path, 47
rituals, 52–55
Scheherazade, ancient goddess, 49–51
sexual nature, 47
Gerhardt, Dana, 7

H
Hestia (Vesta), 81–83
Hippolyta, 28–30
Houston, Jean, 38

I
Inanna, 91–93
Inner Goddess
    awakening, with partner's Inner God, 22
    basic facts about, 18–19
    dealing with moods, 20–21
    pleasure connection, 19–20
    sexual power, 21–22
Isis and Osiris, 25–26

J
Journaling, questions for, 152
Jung, Carl, 20

K
Kenyon, Tom, 21

L
Lacey, Louise, 9
Lakshmi, 39–41
Leo
    activities for when Moon is in, 76–77
    characteristics, 69–70
    greatest strength and weakness, 68
    karmic path, 69
    Oshun, ancient goddess, 70–72
    rituals, 73–76
    sexual nature, 68

Libra
    activities for when Moon is in, 97
    characteristics, 90–91
    greatest strength and weakness, 89
    Inanna, ancient goddess, 91–93
    karmic path, 89
    rituals, 94–96
    sexual nature, 89
Lieber, Arnold, 13
Lilith, 101–103

M
Mary Magdalene, 21
Memories, 18
Mitchell, Edgar, 10
Moon sign, 4
Morrison, Dorothy, 11

N
North, Ora, 101
Northrup, Christiane, 142
Nut and Geb, 25

O
Oshun, 70–72
Osiris and Isis, 25–26

P
Phases of moon
    described, 12–16
    farming and, 10
Pices
    activities for when Moon is in, 150–151
    characteristics, 142, 143
    greatest strength and weakness, 141
    karmic path, 141
    rituals, 146–149
    Sedna, ancient goddess, 142–145
    sexual nature, 141

Purps, Sabine, 29

R
Reflection, questions for, 152
Resources, 153–154
Rhiannon, 133–135
Rituals
    Aquarius, 136–138
    Aries, 31–34
    Cancer, 62–65
    Capricorn, 125–127
    Gemini, 52–55
    Leo, 73–76
    Libra, 94–96
    performing effective, 5
    Pices, 146–149
    Sagittarius, 114–117
    Scorpio, 104–106
    Taurus, 42–45
    Virgo, 85–87

S
Sagittarius
    activities for when Moon is in, 118
    characteristics, 110–111
    Diana, ancient goddess, 111–113
    greatest strength and weakness, 109
    karmic path, 109–110
    rituals, 114–117
    sexual nature, 109
Scheherazade, 49–51
Schrader, Lisa, 80–81
Scorpio
    activities for when Moon is in, 106–107
    characteristics, 100–101
    greatest strength and weakness, 99

    karmic path, 99
    Lilith, ancient goddess, 101–103
    rituals, 104–106
    sexual nature, 99
Sedna, 142–145
Shiva and Shakti, 25
Super Moon, 11

T
Taurus
    activities for when Moon is in, 45
    characteristics, 38–39
    greatest strength and weakness, 37
    karmic path, 37
    Lakshmi, ancient goddess, 39–41
    rituals, 42–45
    sexual nature, 37
Teish, Luisah, 71
Thomashauer, Regena, 19

V
Vesta, 81–83
Virgo
    activities for when Moon is in, 87
    characteristics, 80–81
    greatest strength and weakness, 79
    karmic path, 80
    rituals, 85–87
    sexual nature, 79–80
Vesta, ancient goddess, 81–83

W
Wilcox, Siobhán, 29
Women, Moon as soul mate of, 8–10

CPSIA information can be obtained
at www.ICGtesting.com
Printed in the USA
BVHW060948051022
648637BV00006BA/6